ON HUMAN BEING

Loving & Living Without Purpose

Written by: Carl Bozeman,
Elizabeth, Colorado

ON HUMAN BEING

Other books by Carl Bozeman:

On Being God – Beyond Your Life's Purpose

Are You Listening? Addressing the Divine Within

More information can be found at Carl's website:

www.spiritual-intuition.com

Email: *carl@spiritual-intuition.com*

ON HUMAN BEING

Copyright © 2012 by Carl Bozeman; Denver Colorado
All rights reserved

Printed in the United States of America

No part of this publication may be reproduced, stored in or introduced into a retrieval system, or transmitted, in any form, or by any means (electronic, mechanical, photocopying, recording, or otherwise), without the prior written permission of both the copyright owner and publisher of this book.

The scanning, uploading, and distribution of this book via the internet or via any other means without the permission of the publisher or copyright owner is illegal and punishable by law. Please purchase only authorized electronic editions, and do not participate in or encourage electronic piracy of copyrighted materials. Your support of author's right is appreciated.

Copyright owner website: http://www.spiritual-intuition.com

Table of Contents

CONTRIBUTORS TO THIS BOOK II
FORWARD III
INTRODUCTION V
COSMIC TRAIN 11
DISEMBARK; PLANET EARTH 23
COSMIC STORYTELLING 35
FAITH – OUR MYTHOLOGICAL PARTNER 47
EMOTIONS; TREES AND HUMAN BARK 55
COSMIC DECEPTION 73
WHAT'S HAPPENING? 81
DUALITY – MONITORING YOUR ILLUSION 93
SAVIORISM; CAN YOU REALLY BE SAVED? 109
CREATIVE RESPONSIBILITY 117
STREAM OF LIFE 125
AFTERWORD 136

Contributors to this Book

Contributors to this book are many. Literally everyone who has been a part of my life experience directly or indirectly has played a role in the creation of this book. I could not be where I am now nor could I have written these words had it not been for each and every one of you including those reading right now. I thank you for allowing me to be a part of your experience. These are not my words; they are yours.

Forward

I said to my soul, be still and wait without hope, for hope would be hope for the wrong thing; wait without love, for love would be love of the wrong thing; there is yet faith, but the faith and the love and the hope are all in the waiting. Wait without thought, for you are not ready for thought: So the darkness shall be the light, and the stillness the dancing. ~ T. S. Eliot

Introduction

As I look upon the layered blue waters separated by the uneven lines of foaming white waves breaking onto the California coastline I am moved at such beauty but saddened that this will be the last time I see it. The short flight from Santa Barbara to Los Angeles to visit three of my four children lets me reflect on my troubled life. This is the last time I will see them and that they will see me. Later I will travel to Seattle to see my fourth child to say goodbye to him as well. They won't know it is goodbye. All they will know is how much I love them, how much they have meant to me and how very proud I am of each of them. Their memory of me will be the pleasant time we spend together these next few days.

My marriage is over. I alone have wrecked it in every way and broken the woman I adored above all others. My infidelity, mental illness and erratic nature have ended what was once my greatest comfort and relationship with my best friend. I ponder my life as a child growing up in Tacoma, Washington with six sisters in a house too small to contain us. My father leaving abruptly at the age of seven and without any reason that I comprehended and, whom, I would not see or hear from for over fifty years. I consider the embarrassment of poverty and destitution that immediately befell us upon his leaving. How everything spun out of control and neighbors, relatives and my very own mother transformed into monsters who would abuse me physically, mentally and sexually. How my best friend, an older gentleman and neighbor would break the trust of innocence and sexually abuse me while crying and begging me to forgive him. A tear runs down my cheek as I recall those awful times. It is all I remember but not for long, I tell myself.

I reflect on my years as a father, husband and provider to my own family and all the activities I participated in with them so they could have what I could not. How I had protected them from the ugliness I had known when I was a child. I was dedicated to them and to my wife who stood with me as the demons of my past percolated into my awareness. I was a mess and I tried to protect my family from my own suffering and sadness but I could not. I would pour myself into over twenty five years of therapy and medication and an endless search to find that one moment in a cruel past that would set the demons free and free me from the depression, post-traumatic stress and multiple personalities I suffered from. It would never happen. The moment would not come and so I would bring it all to an end myself. As I sat aboard that airplane, looking down, I felt relief but not freedom. Freedom would come later. A sudden but quiet end to misery, suffering and the unanswered question: Why?

While visiting my three children in Los Angeles we had decided to go to a late night movie that would start a few hours later but were unsure how to pass time until then. We were gathered at my oldest son's apartment where we chose a DVD to watch, which, we all agreed would be a good means to kill time until it was time to go to the theatre. I was in an easy place and I was calm and relaxed. The struggle was soon to be over and knowing this gave me great peace. There was nothing else to do but have fun and enjoy this short time with my children. Then it happened.

Suddenly, I felt myself lifting out of my body in a most unsettling way. I hovered just above my children and myself and watched them, and me, watching the movie. I felt the lightness of this strange state and there was a purity to it that made me feel the cleanest I had ever felt. I was completely given over to what I was in that state and no longer felt any connection, whatsoever, to the person sitting in the chair as the physical me. In an instant I was swept up into an awareness that the human before me was not who I was. I was, clearly, not that body and despite all the suffering that that body had been through there was nothing that would alter this exhilarating new perception of who I was. I could see that I was not the experiences of my physical body rather I now knew I was the "experiencer" of my physical body.

This recognition completely washed away everything I held as significant and causal in making the decision to end my life. None of what I perceived myself to be when that decision was made existed anymore and I realized, in that moment I truly was free. This new sense of freedom opened me up and everything about my existence changed. Who I truly am was trapped in a human body whose only awareness was human experience and all the human could do to stop it was to end the physical life. All that went away. I now saw something far beyond the human identity I had become and all my perceptions of what used to be changed in a way that became grand and wonderful. As this "I" settled back into my physical body I knew I was not what I once believed myself to be and I saw life, intelligence oozing in everything and it took my breath away! The double sidedness of everything, I once experienced, physically, ended. There was nothing that was not magnificent and in that magnificence all things blended into each other.

Soon thereafter I left my marriage of thirty two years, stopped all anti-depressant medications, ended all therapy, quit my job and career and began to write, which is what I continue to do. I was saved in a moment of despair and complete release of all worldly things and literally freed from darkness.

The title of this book is "On Human Being – Loving & Living Without Purpose." It is a book about "tip toeing through humanity and walking lightly leaving most of what we find along the way intact and without our markings upon it. It is about finding the inner self that sojourns for a little while and returns to whatever cosmic reality we come from. It is about rethinking what we think! Actually, it is about replacing our thinking with spontaneous action that boils up from somewhere inside. It is about the discovery of our unique and innate natures as divine beings. This is a book that reinforces that our unique human experience already is the purpose!

Carl Bozeman

Chapter 1

Cosmic Train

Earth life is a vacation from the cosmic train we all ride on through our infinite existence. It is a unique experience all of us who choose to visit get to enjoy, if we accept that the only reason we are here is to enjoy. It may seem erroneous to consider that we are here to experience three dimensional reality as a vacation or as something we should enjoy when we see so much pain, suffering and sorrow in the world. The reality of existence here on earth is that it is nothing in comparison to our existence in eternity. We are no less infinite on earth than we are in eternity.

While aboard the cosmic train, a few of us have gotten off here at earth and as we pass through the gates of birth, we enter a new kind of awareness that overwhelms everything else we once knew. The old awareness gets tucked away but is always there. We sense that there is more to us, but in the new earthly awareness, it is difficult to hold onto and pull it into this reality. Some do and we see them as mysterious and unique, but never allow that, we too, are just as they are. Earthly awareness is so tactile and sensory. The stimuli we take in through our earthly senses overwhelms us in a sea of experience and richness that is difficult to separate from the reality of who we truly are. So we are driven to find answers in this reality to that mysterious knowing we have about ourselves that is bigger than our means of communication can express. We look for meaning and purpose in terms of what we see and in the expressions we communicate, but even with all of that, we are sometimes left empty. The search continues.

The purposes of life are explored and examined but the answers we seek lay hidden.

There really is no purpose in this life other than to experience reality as only humans can. Every aspect of life should be embraced and we should revel in every minute of it regardless of whether we judge the experience good or bad. Our purpose, if there is any purpose, is to live and live abundantly in the richness of sensory experiences our human existence allows. Our existence "is" the meaning of life! Living "it" is its only purpose. However, it is ours to choose how we let the sensory awareness of this life be measured. We can choose to embrace it and enjoy all its ups and downs, or we can be miserable as we slog our way through it to our death, or the entrance back on the cosmic train we disembarked from. We make it what it is and we can blame no one for our experience. Sure, our innate nature has been masked, but it is not unknowable. We live according to our awareness and that is as it should be. That is what we came here for; therefore, every minute of earthly awareness should be basked in for its wonderful and delicious sensory experience.

The search for a greater meaning or purpose to life is in some ways its own problem. It suggests that we cannot be here for any other reason than to embrace and enjoy everything about life. It leads us to question our lives and the experience we have as meaningful in ways that they are not meant to be. It adds seriousness to our existence that drives us to meanings that can only make sense in this reality but do not begin to address our own innate knowing that we are so much more than what we sense in this existence, or than what language will allow us to describe. That is a lot about what this existence is about - coming to grips with the limitations of awareness and communication we otherwise have as gods. There is no way we can describe our divine nature in the languages of humans, but we are not supposed to. Remember we are on vacation and compared to our divine nature, the pace here on earth is slowed down considerably. Our infinite state is a quickened state in which our awareness is of things incomprehensible in this life... earth life is seriously slowed down. In fact, our own human-ness slows us down even more.

For instance, it has been proven scientifically that our bodies, including what we call our physical senses, take in sensory input, several billion bits of information every second, and yet what we are capable of being conscious of is in the range of twenty to thirty bits per second. Something about this experience as humans filters out so much of what goes on that what we are conscious of is infinitesimal to what is really happening. When we consider our divine or spiritual natures, the information we receive is even greater than what we experience on the human level. In fact, our spiritual sensitivity is so finely tuned it is barely detectable and in most scientific circles, it is nonexistent simply because we do not have the three dimensional means to detect it. What is not detectable in this reality is usually left to speculation, theory or is just relegated as non-existent. Even though most of us at one time or another have felt something in ourselves that is more far-reaching than we can articulate, if we cannot define it, or measure it, it cannot be, or so says our science.

Human consciousness or sub consciousness is not the extent of our experience. We have built in conditions and filters that sift through the enormous amount of information, bombarding us every second, which screen out the majority of our experience. This is what I mean when I refer to life as an illusion in my book <u>On Being God</u>. What makes it into our conscious awareness is what we have been conditioned or programmed to know and accept. Most of us have heard that when the Spanish ships appeared on the horizon upon discovering the "New World", the inhabitants could not see them. There was nothing in their conditioning that could explain what they saw and yet intuitively they saw something. Their programming simply could not identify it and nothing in their experience, other than clouds, could the ships on the horizon be compared to.

We know it took the shamans of those native people several days to come up with a description they could then convey to the rest of the people. Only then could they identify this new phenomenon and only then could they put this new description into their own language and make it part of their experience. Consider how much is going by us if in every second of life, billions and billions of images, sounds, smells, tastes, touches and any number of sensory inputs we can't possibly remember get discarded by processes we barely understand. Life goes on around us at light speed but we only sense it at a snail's pace. And the civilizing of ourselves, as we refer to it, is only slowing it down even more. Think about what is passing us by.

In the early 1990's, I worked for a telecommunications company whose products helped optimize the available bandwidth of copper phone lines around the world. Cellular technology was in its infancy as was fiber optics, so maximizing the available telephone bandwidth was of major importance because there were only so many copper lines available to an ever increasing population of telephone users. The product we developed was a device that would convert an analog voice signal to a digital signal, remove any extraneous noise such as the static or ambient noise one often heard on a telephone land line, and then packetize the cleaned up digital signal into small packets that would be sent across the line to another device that would assemble the packets, convert the digital signal to an analog signal and, wonder of wonder, a voice was heard speaking just as on any phone call.

What was so unique about this product, for the time, was that in processing calls in such a way and by eliminating all the extraneous noise, we could put sixteen voice conversations across a telephone line that up to that time could only carry one, representing a huge savings to businesses who were paying for multiple lines at great cost as well as a serious improvement to the usage of the available bandwidth.

One of the interesting facets of developing this technology was the idea that the extraneous noise in normal telephone conversations carried no useful information and could be removed without any affect to those speaking and those listening. Little did our developers know that the noise did provide one very important piece of information.

All of us who have used the old land line telephones always had a sense that our call was viable because we could hear the noise of the connection during breaks in the conversation. The information carried by the noise was that the call was still connected. Even though the noise adds nothing to the words spoken or heard, it did add to the assurance that in between words spoken and words heard the line was still connected. When we removed that assurance, sure enough, people who used the new technology complained that during the breaks in a conversation, the line went so silent they couldn't tell if the connection was still intact. The familiar noise of land line conversations was a carrier of information that, like so much in our reality, is taken for granted but missed if it is gone.

We are missing more and more in our reality due to the stripping away of the noise of life that civilization, culture, and upbringing filters out, and the absence of it is causing us to be aware of less but to seek more. In other words, we are starving ourselves of the richness of life in all its forms and replacing it with the illusions of culture and civilization that have been drained of nutrients necessary to the soul. Our aloneness in the world stems not from the isolation we feel from our brothers and sisters. It stems from the filtering of life that has isolated us from our own god-ness and that of everyone else. That is what we seek in life – not human connection, but divine connection. Individually and societally, we are crying out more and more for something to fill our satiated souls, and more and more civilization devises empty stimulation to keep us in control – in check from venturing away from the illusion we know.

The illusion we live, like the processed foods we eat, have been stripped of those things that would enrich and nourish us and replaced with fillers and synthetic nutrients that satisfy temporarily but do not fill us. Our connections to nature have been replaced with television, radio, internet and other civilized forms of media that have been carefully engineered to play to an illusory beat we have all been taken in by. Like the packetizing of small pieces of digitized voice from a telephone call, information is carefully fed to us at a rate not to exceed our ability to pay attention. So much of the information is stripped away that we only get teased with what is really happening and before we have a chance to try to figure out what information has been stripped away, we are hit with another perfectly timed, perfectly sized packet of seriously reduced information.

The illusion is so complete that we, as participators in it, have accepted slogans such as "give them what they want" believing that what we want is what we are being given. Meanwhile, for those who search for greater awareness, getting outside of the illusion is extremely difficult and so they search in vain among the institutions of civilization for the soul nourishment they crave.

What was intended to be a stopping off point, a vacation from other awareness has now become a desperate struggle to somehow survive natural forces that, while once were so much a part of us, have now become the enemy. Our illusion of what this reality is has become so synthesized that we have replaced what was always intended – enjoyment, enrichment, tranquility and nourishment - with a struggle fraught with peril, tragedy and synthetic stimulation. Our cosmic vacation has become so empty, so stressful that we now look for ways to vacation from the vacation! And where do we go? To those places with as little civilization as possible. We go to those places where we can rest, soak up the sun, or be inspired by the beauty of a natural wonder such as a mountain, a river, the ocean or a canyon. We sometimes go to the civilized, manmade attractions but, while fun and stimulating; they often leave us empty and un-refreshed.

The oldest among us recall fondly the quieter and less hectic times they grew up in and the freedoms they enjoyed then that are so distant now. The youngest of us cannot even conceive of these things they describe. The sterilizing manner of civilization removes the adventure and connectedness to the world whose intention it was all along to enrich us and enliven us from an infinite "other world" reality. Our souls came here for enrichment, not our bodies, and yet it is our bodies that our civilized world caters to. The experience of life has become a race, a competition to find purpose and meaning by indulging the senses in every possible way, such that the soul is lost completely to the gratification of the physical or three dimensional aspect of our lives. We hear the statement that "we are spiritual beings having a physical experience". Yes, we are having a physical experience, but not to the extent that we completely overshadow our spiritual nature.

In the Old Testament, there is a story of the man Job whom most have heard of in some form or another. The story of Job is the story of a man who has everything this life can offer. He is a man of great wealth, influence and notable character. He is God-fearing and righteous and is blessed with a large family, creature comforts, as we call them and the respect of everyone in his country. Job's story takes a bizarre twist as Satan convinces God to let him break Job and show God that if he were to lose all the things in life he possesses, that Job would lose his faith and curse God. God allows Satan to literally take everything from Job including his family, wealth, and good fortune. Satan is even allowed to cause great scourges and illness to come upon Job, but Job, while physically broken in every way, never forsakes his faith, nor does he turn against God. Job does, however, question why one as righteous as he, is treated so poorly by the God he worships. He even asks God to take his life and end his misery. Job suffers all that is thrown at him, but never accepts that he is evil or that God is punishing him for some act he has committed. Job does seek for answers to his suffering and requests to speak to God face to face. God grants Job's request and appears to him as a whirlwind.

It is extremely interesting God's response to Job and very relevant to our experience here in this life. Instead of speaking in any way to Job about his suffering, God directs Job to look all around and take in all the beauty and wonder he is surrounded by. God covers every aspect of creation and life on this earth and not once addresses Job as a sinful man or in a way Job desires. All manner of creatures are mentioned as well as the wind, rain, water, snow, hail and frost. It can be taken that God rules over everything and is greater than all things but it is as if God is trying to show Job that the things that are naturally here on earth are what is important in life. All of it is here for the good of our souls and yet our so called civilizing or taming of nature is not unlike that of Job questioning God why he is made to suffer.

How is it that we can suppose that the egoic cravings of humans can nourish our starving souls when any of it has no comparison, whatsoever, to the beauty, majesty and abundance of this earth? The treasures of life are not found in the creations of man. They are found in the raw creative beauty of which we are all a part. When we see that eagle soar high above and we gasp for breath as we watch, "we" are every bit as breath-taking and none of it is because we have created our cities, monuments, and wonders. It is because our souls, like the eagles, soar above everything we believe important and look down on something so vast and wonderful. Nothing in our creative imagining comes close to its splendor.

We are the recipients of this splendor. No act or outcome in this life will change the nature of our soul in the eternities. Nothing we do here matters, so all that we need do here is embrace everything that goes on, every experience, every accomplishment, and every aspect of the life we live should be embraced in every possible way as another part of our vacation. None of us should ever feel we are victims of circumstance when we step back on to that cosmic train. We should be refreshed, invigorated, uplifted and alive from a richness of experience we may never know again, and while in infinite terms the experience is a blip on the cosmic screen, every part of this experience should leave us absolutely vibrating. What a gift it is to be here and to experience the incredible highs and lows of humankind. We should relish every moment of it.

Too many can't wait, like Job of old, to get out of life and back on board the train. Life has not been the pleasure trip it was meant to be, but that is only because in the egoic life we live and try to fit into, we lose sight of why we are here. As God spoke to Job and asked him to identify one thing in his experience that remotely compared to the splendor of this planet and everything on it, Job shrank before Him and could not. The reason is that there is no manmade thing that compares to anything on earth and in infinite terms, nothing on earth including earth itself compares to our lives in eternity.

In the last chapter of Job, the epitaph, Job is restored to his health, position, and stature that he knew before Satan physically broke him. In fact, it was greater than before. The story of Job is a metaphor for us here on earth living life that regardless of our circumstances or how we view our life experience, in the end we are restored to our unique and divine situation. If we learn to see this life, our experience, as God instructed Job to view it, nothing else matters. Nothing we do or accomplish in this life will ever surpass just being a part of life here on earth in whatever form it takes. The cosmic train leaves no one behind regardless of how the earth experience went for them. Like Job, we are all restored back to that infinite reality we all exist in. We won't be looking back as in infinity, all things blend together into one big whole, and it is wondrous. All of it is wondrous!

Life and living are the only reason we are here and all of it is to be enjoyed, but only as you choose. We cannot fail at life! There really are no illusions, only the ones we choose to accept as our condition. We can change everything in our experience here in this life and we should because we get back onboard the cosmic train all too soon.

Chapter 2

Disembark; Planet Earth

Who stepped off the "Cosmic Train" is a daunting unknowing that only grows larger when we look into the night sky and see the darkness filled with tiny distant lights and ponder our unique existence in such a vast universe. We ask, "Are we alone or will we ever be able to travel such incredible distances to explore and search for others like us, or not like us?" It is a compelling, but complex mystery that challenges even the greatest scientific minds because of the inherent inability of the mind to comprehend infinity. In our lives on earth we grow to like the solidity and order of everything in our experience. Looking out into the heavens or considering infinity disrupts that order. We turn to science or religion for answers but no one can ever completely remove the mystery that surrounds our presence here...our not knowing, as it were. We may never know who stepped off that train and we will certainly never agree from a collective human viewpoint.

All we may ever be able to come to terms with in this life is that we are here and that we are unique. We seem to get that. Our own science tells us that at a basic energetic level we and everything else are the same even though we can see that we are uniquely different from other humans, other life forms and all the various forms we encounter in existence. No two things in any form of nature are exactly the same in appearance yet in our energetic make up there is no difference other than the rate at which energy vibrates. So what accounts for that uniqueness if everything is the same at the basic elemental level? Again, another mystery we may never comprehend in this reality; or will we? In the book "On Being God -

Beyond Your Life's Purpose" we are told that most of what we perceive in life is an illusion of the conditioned mind we acquire as we are taught and trained throughout our lives. That conditioning is what upholds our perception of reality even though we know so much more is going on that we are not perceptively aware of. In other words, the level of our awareness is responsible for the level of our illusion of reality. We perceive what we have accepted as reality and yet none of us accepts, or live as though, we are all the same. All things that are said to be equal do not appear to be equal. How, then, do we account for all the variety in life?

Science has developed ideas and theories about our existence and our unique selves but science tends to only consider observable facts in a strictly three dimensional sense. If it cannot be observed in these terms it is not included in the base of knowledge we claim to have about life, existence and all the other things happening. What this means is that the character and personality of humans comes from genetics, environment and other measurable phenomenon we tend to be aware of. Everything else is ruled out because it is too abstract and doesn't fit the scientific framework for proper investigation. This while knowing that things are going on far outside our ability to observe them. Such things may possibly never be understood. Science will only study what it can measure and while science attempts to imagine things outside the box of three dimensional reality it has no imagination outside it. The truth is that we will never understand the differences between humans or any other living or non-living thing in a scientific way; not fully anyway. That is because there is no way to study spiritual things unless they somehow fall into emotional or psychological areas but that is not likely. Spiritual things fall outside physically measurable norms, but most of us on some level know that there is more to us than what we see. These subtle, but real, knowing's remind us that we are part of something that is much greater than what is visible on the surface. In fact, many of us recognize coincidences and find meaning in their happening but fail to recognize that they only seem to be coincidence because they happen so infrequently. Coincidences for most of us are an infrequent look through the keyhole at a spiritual realm that is interwoven into every aspect of our lives. If we could unlock the door instead of looking through just the keyhole we would see worlds without number, others moving in and out of our reality in such a way it would startle the mind that can only see three dimensionally. We are living in a much more complex, interwoven reality than our awareness, religion, or science comprehends but we are conditioned not to see it. The question that may be asked, "So what is going on?" We have all heard the saying that we are spiritual beings having a physical experience but we live as though we are physical beings trying to become spiritual. It should be exactly the opposite. If we truly are spiritual, and we are, then it is a regression of the spiritual nature we all possess when becoming human. We have the whole scenario backwards with our ideas of purpose and meaning and that we must search to the ends of the earth to find that purpose. We live as though the search for purpose and meaning is how we find our spiritual path but it is really the opposite. We are already spiritual! Becoming human is going down from being high, not the reverse. We live life trying to work up when everything points to working down. Down should not be construed as bad or a reversal of our godlike nature but more a slowing down the pace of living as gods.

Life might be thought of as a vacation from the work of being gods on such a grand scale. Life on earth is greatly simplified from life at the speed of light – or the speed of gods, whatever that might be. We are spiritual, divine creatures taking on human form and experiencing that in a way only gods can but we live as though we must prove something here as humans in order to get back to a heavenly presence we all seem to have forgotten. We look at human existence as a lowly existence and create gods so great that we struggle the rest of our lives trying to measure up to what we already are! As gods already all we ever have to do is to embrace the human experience and simply enjoy it. You cannot attain what you already are, and we are all gods who have created this unique experience for ourselves and no one else.

Settle down and settle into the experience of human life instead of falling into the trap that we must work up to something that just isn't in play with the human existence. Get busy being human and enjoy it. Embrace every aspect of it and stop worrying about what you have forgotten about your divine nature. It will all come back if not in this life then for sure in the next one, whatever that may be. The human experience is part of a much larger happening we, as gods, are involved in. In fact, it is a happening we have created for our own benefit and it is of no benefit to run ourselves ragged trying to find some profound and significant meaning to our lives. That we are living is the meaning and as unglamorous as that may sound it is significant!

Most of us accept the uniqueness of the individuals we encounter in this life. We hear it spoken that no two people are alike but when we get to the realm of parenting this idea breaks down. Most parents will define a set of rules and guidelines that each child must conform to or else be dealt with appropriately. We are told that children need boundaries but how often do we recognize that boundaries for one may be anathema to another? We watch the frustration of parents as they struggle to get everyone of their children to conform to the same set of rules. We comment about how one child is the perfect angel while another won't do a thing we say.

As children grow we see their unique personalities and characteristics emerge and while we recognize those unique aspects the rules almost seem too tighten. Also, we see the influence of institutions begin to have an effect and, of course, if the boundaries and rules of those institutions are violated the consequences vary all the way up to expulsion or entry into new institutions designed especially for those who do not conform. While most seem to make it through this, almost every adult can look back at a time as a child where their confinement was really an internment and violated their idea of freedom. Children live life with abandoned but are systematically conditioned to live a life of purpose that is best suited for them as concluded by the collective. We even say things like "living life on purpose" and yet our parenting and institutional guidance seems to frown on any purpose that does not fit some set of rules that fit within certain boundaries.

It is unfortunate that we have gone this way since children are closer to who it is they truly are then virtually any adult will ever be. Nevertheless we structure their lives and condition them away from the knowing that they are divine. Sad to think that as they are pulled further and further away from their divine awareness, so too, are we. Few adults will not admit they are uplifted in a very special way when in the presence of a newborn baby or very young children. Additionally, adults will almost never contemplate why they feel this way. What is it in a child that pulls us toward a divine sense of awareness? How often do we hear at the birth of a child that it is a miracle?

Still we begin immediately to reshape these miracles into what we have come to accept is important in life and as they grow older the light we all notice at first is drained out of them just as it has for us. Few like to admit this but this is how it is. We teach our children to be conforming and dull. Not to be alert to the mystery of life. Alertness has nothing to do with awareness of present conditions and circumstances as we are all taught. Alertness is really being aware of what is not directly in front of our eyes. We are all born with such awareness and we are alert to it until it is replaced with what is believed to be more important.

In essence we are two individuals while sojourning here on earth. Broken down to our most basic selves there is the spiritual or god who has come to occupy the other part which is the human. The personality or character of the spiritual has always existed and is in no way connected to the genetics or environment of the human. That personality always emerges and while we would like everything to be ordered and structured the soul's personality is unique and profound and will remain that way forever. The sole basis for our experience here on earth is for the spiritual to experience the human. For many spiritually minded people we have entered a time when life must have a purpose and we drive ourselves to find it while we have somehow forgotten that our unique human form is the purpose. We have it all backwards. We look for purpose when our being here is the purpose.

If environment and conditioning is what is responsible for our personality then it is responsible to assume that we could provide the conditions and environments to have two people be exactly the same. But we can't. We know this. We can't even produce identical characteristics in identical twins. Every personality emerges on its own regardless of the conditions it is brought up in.

We see this in the lives of so many of our great, iconic leaders and teachers throughout the ages.

For instance Siddhartha was of royal dissent. Privilege beyond all others and certainly his conditioning was such that he would rule kingdoms of men as a royal. His education must have been the best that could be had and his life of privilege must have been a life others of lower class would have aspired to. In fact, it is believed that he was sheltered from everything going on outside his royal life so that he would never question that how he lived was not normal for everyone. Still, despite all his status, fortune and privilege his innate personality, his unique and divine nature had to manifest itself. For some reason as he looked at the world outside his own he recognized that the majority of people did not have anything like the life he knew. This tore at his soul to such an extent that he gave up everything he knew to live a beggar's life and be among his fellow humans among whom he was raised to be superior.

What called him to such a life that was so compelling that he would give up wealth and privilege and the very things we are conditioned to aspire to now? We are told constantly that having more frees us to be able to do and give more. We are constantly pointed toward those who have such things as Siddhartha walked away from in order to have what has come to be termed "the successful life and yet we look to him as one of the greatest of all humans having existed. In our aspirations and pursuits of what He walked away from, even now we tend to overlook what a journey it must've been for him to become the first Buddha. Instead we look at him as the Buddha and call him great and wonderful and yet if he were here now, he himself would not recognize such greatness.

The Buddha is just one example of the emergence of the personality, the god within us in spite of our conditioning to the contrary. There are so many others whom we have made famous, holy or inspiring but the greatness we credit all of our icons with is no different than what each of us possess as well. In fact, it is likely that our greatest struggles in life are the result of our human conditioning that opposes our innate, divine natures.

There are studies in the United States and likely in other countries that upwards of seventy percent of the working population are unhappy with their jobs or careers. It is probably greater than that. What does this tell us about our conditioning as humans? From the moment of our birth when everyone who observes us and is lifted up by our divine and miraculous nature we are told what is important in life. We are convinced through constant conditioning that education, career, credentials and so much more is what is important in life and we are somehow convinced that we must give up certain things to get ahead.

Getting ahead is what is important and to do so we must sometimes sacrifice an innate knowing we have inside that says otherwise. If seventy percent of the working population is unhappy with their careers how happy can they otherwise be? If the purpose of life is to enjoy the experience of living as a spiritual being having a human experience wouldn't a thirty percent or less success rate be a strong indicator that something is wrong?

It is widely believed that much of the disease and illness in the world today is caused from stress in life including the work environment. There are many descriptions of stress and ideas of how it is induced but ultimately it is the result of the rift between what the human form has been conditioned to believe and what our unique spiritual nature is. In other words, what we have come to believe is important at the physical level is fighting against the spiritual. The physical self tears at the spiritual self. It is a denial of the divine, the god that you are, and it sickens the body to the point of early failure. Stress is talked about a great deal these days and it should begin to become apparent that something about the way we have been conditioned and the way we condition our children is creating enmity between the spiritual and the human form. So much so that we are creating an epidemic of stress and bodily failure in the process.

We are taught from birth to replace what we innately are with what we are not. Parents seek every advantage they can to steer their children from their innate nature to what their particular conditioning says is important. Children grow up and struggle trying to be what parents and society say they should be. How could children not struggle? Their teeth are set on edge every time they are instructed to go against their innate nature and seek out careers or lifestyles that are more suited to the illusion we have accepted as an abundant life.

Most of us are no longer alert to what is really going on. We are very aware of what goes on directly in front of our eyes but outside that awareness we are not alert to our placement in the more expansive nature of things going on around us. It's like I can see what you are doing, but I cannot see why you are doing it." Or "I see things happening in front of me but I cannot see the effect they are having on all things I don't see." As already mentioned alertness has nothing to do with what is directly in view of our physical senses. It has to do with simply being aware that mystery surrounds us far beyond anything we sense physically. Alertness puts us in to the spectrum of mystery which is the largest part of our experience even though we are unaware in the physical sense.

   To illustrate this I had an experience with my father that made me so much more aware of the bigger picture than I had ever imagined. He fell one night and was rushed to the hospital where he was non responsive to normal physical stimulus. I had seen this sort of thing before with him and told the emergency room doctors that he simply needed to sleep some and after a little rest he would wake up and be as ornery as ever. I began to worry when, after about sixteen hours, he was non-responsive and of course the doctors were saying his situation was very dire. At the point I began to give up hope of ever speaking to him again he came around, just as I expected originally. When that happened I went back to my learned awareness that he would have these little spells but would come back as he always had before. His condition improved so he was moved to a room inside the hospital where he could be observed and cared for but without the emergency room critical care since his condition was no longer considered dire.

   We had a wonderful time for the next two days while he was kept under observation and all monitoring of vital signs indicated he was perfectly healthy. On the second day of observation he insisted I take his ring which he always wore on his left hand ring finger even though he and my mother were divorced and he had never remarried. I thought it was unusual in a way but in his old age I accepted it as just another quirky aspect of his aging personality. In handing me the ring he insisted that it had power and would protect me. I took the ring and told him I would keep it with me always which brought a smile and a nod of approval from him. We spent the rest of the day visiting and preparing him for his return to his home the next morning as he was given a clean bill of health and was signed out of the hospital's care.

He died early the next morning a few hours after I had left to return home. I was completely taken by surprise as was the hospital staff. My alertness was only aware of the information I could physically see in front of me. It was the same for all the medical staff assigned to observe and assist him. All any of us could see is the physical monitoring. None of us could see that death was swallowing him up. He, however, knew it and gave me those last two days to help me be aware of it but I was so caught up in my perception of reality that I failed to comprehend that none of what was happening was about me in any way. I was unable to see the mystery unfolding in front of me even as he was imploring me to take his ring and keep it with me always as his gesture of protecting me even after he would be gone. It was all right there in front of me. The infinite into which my Father was passing surrounded me on every side and in every way and all I could see was the physical nature of things playing out in a very superficial way. All I could make of the mysterious events playing out was "My Daddy is coming home and all would be as it formerly was."

When I look back on, what was then, a sad time I can see how completely I was surrounded in mystery and that extraneous events were pressing on me to awaken to something far more profound than what I was sensing as just a human. What happened with my father in those few short hours, was about everything seen and unseen. Mystery and physical perception; alertness is awareness of both. What we think of as mundane is wrapped in mystery but we are so busy in our world of details and routine that mystery slips quietly by.

Who we are has nothing to do with what we think. In fact, exactly the opposite is true. Who we are is what we do not think and those coincidental life experiences we all encounter from time to time are clearer expressions of what our reality is. They are also pointers to the underlying "who" that we are underneath the physical "I" we are taught to believe we are. You are unimaginable; we all are. The finite cannot comprehend the infinite and so our human expressions, intended to define us, do nothing more than limit us.

Who you are knows no physical bounds, whatsoever. The whispers of other worlds, other realities seep into our awareness when we let go of all ideas that tell us we are our physical bodies; our minds, our egos. On the other side of physical-ness lies the real you and best of all; you have always been there!

Chapter 3

Cosmic Storytelling

The common thread in all our lives is the similarities of myths throughout all of human history and within every civilization that attests that we all have a common awareness that permeates us regardless of how we are conditioned. The most common myth is that we all look to transcend our own mortality. We believe there is something greater than what we see in this existence. Our souls yearn for it and so throughout the ages, we have created our gods in such a way that they know the way of transcendence. It is as if we are all programmed from the very beginning of this earthly existence to ask the same questions about where we came from, why we are here, and what lies beyond. It is as if the gods hard wired us to ask such questions to constantly remind us that we are greater than anything we can conceive of, as three dimensional brings. We are constantly being tweaked by these questions as if to always have a door through which we can go, but only when we are ready. The great difficulty is being able to rise above the reality we have come to accept outside that door. Our attachment to life, or what we have been conditioned to see as life, is what prevents us from pushing the door open and walking through. Our acceptance of the terms and conditions of this life is what prevents us from getting the answers to those questions we ask, and yet we continue to ask them and look for ways to find answers that do not violate the rules of three dimensional reality as we know it.

We are asked to have faith that a particular path will get us to that higher "existence" we all seem to sense within. Somehow, however, we can't quite accept the idea that the substance of those things we hope for becomes the evidence of those things we cannot see. How difficult it is to be asked to believe that which we cannot see and to live in such a way that we must trust those who think they know better. How do we connect the evidence of our seeing with the hopes of things we once had before and how long must we wait and trust in the idea that comes to us from others whom we have convinced ourselves we must? Are we left to always wonder when the evidence we seek never comes?

The myths of man are a portal, a way to look, not from the inside out but from the outside in. The basic nature of all humans to know their inner essence is the evidence of our own connectedness to all of life. Mythology is an outgrowth of that which we see and don't see, but it has a basis in each one of us at a deep inner level that forces us to ask, what everyone asks, and to search for greater insight into our own divine nature. It is the common link in all of us that tries to answer the deeper questions of our existence that our three dimensional reality cannot. The twists and turns our myths take are all attempts to make that which is mortal, immortal. In other words, we are somehow raised from this plane to another by forces stronger than us.

Mortality is a constant for all of us and the idea that we all die is imposing. Not so much that we die physically in this life, but that in dying there is nothing else. Our greatest fear is that nothing more exists beyond this life and so the questions. We somehow understand that our lives, as we know them, are not all there is, but we are so thoroughly conditioned that we question everything we know at deeper levels and great fear arises because we have forgotten that we are infinite and continue on forever in some form.

Mythology gives us a basis to grab onto something outside the reality we have come to accept for ourselves and provide a nugget of hope that what we see and are is not all there is. We know innately that we are more than what is manifest here in this reality. We know this on so many levels and in so many ways, but our ultimate fear that this is all there is freezes us and lets us swim forever in a sea of doubt. Do I look at myself and wonder if I am greater than all of this or do I blindly accept that I can be what I am when I follow a prescribed outline created by the formulation of one particular interpretation of myth we all seem to know? The unknown is daunting and yet we all seem to know that there is so much more to the human creature then meets the three dimensional eye.

Our myths provide possibilities for those looming questions we ask from the depth our souls and attempts to do it in a way that makes sense in three dimensional terms, which is how we are all conditioned to be. We like the tidiness of answers when they fit into the reality we all exist in while here on earth. We are comforted when things can be proved scientifically or observationally, but we also tend to be drawn to the abstract ideas that our myths preserve in us. Somehow the gods, as in Greek mythology, provide us a sense of wonder, possibility and drama that exceeds the routines of everyday living. We like to think that our gods will pity us when down-trodden, protect us when in danger, or uphold us when in doubt. We want to know that something or someone out there has all these powers and uses them kindly and wisely to our benefit. There is security in giving over this kind of power to something greater than us and in letting ourselves be cared for by such power.

Mythology gives context and substance to our own letting go of what we truly are. Thank goodness for our myths because they have kept us connected to the idea of greatness and power even though we have forgotten that the power we give our mythic heroes and gods is our own power. We are the heroes of all mythology! There are no heroes outside what we are and when we decide to see that in ourselves is when we begin to understand that the greatness of life only exists because of "our own" greatness.

Our mythologies take on weird and wonderful twists and turns and we sometimes wonder what the gods are doing? It is this sense of wonder, perplexity and drama that attracts many of us to the plight of them. However, in spite of all the oddities of our unique cultural myths, they all remain surprisingly similar regardless of the culture. They all represent profound strength and uniqueness regardless of their origin and they are the servers of goodness, mercy and justice. We call upon them for whatever earthly needs we think we have. We credit them for all we have in this existence, and while we ascribe to them all this power to control and affect our lives, the real power lies within us individually. Their mythology is our own mythology and any power we ascribe to our heroes, gods and villains is our own power.

As long as we continue to accept the illusion of our existence, there will be myths. We cannot exist without them because it is they that keep us connected to the reality of life which is beyond everything we believe about ourselves and life on this planet. There is a greater part of us that, while mostly hidden, transcends all of our illusory beliefs. Our myths are the "voice crying in the wilderness" that allow us to, if only to fantasize, be something we just can't seem to grasp while in this life. Consequently, what we believe about ourselves, our mythological beliefs, is what we project to an outside world whose citizens do the same both individually and collectively. How we sell ourselves to others and the world is through our myths. That is why they all seem so similar.

All of us wonder about what or who we are, how we came to be and what happens after. Myths provide the link between those questions of wonderment and our current place in reality, and even though we sometimes institutionalize them, we all seem to know there is something else beyond them. Mythology does not seem to solve the "we" about "us" meaning that while the characters of our myths are individualized, the myths themselves are encompassing of the societies to which they relate. While we cannot allow ourselves to be as the gods and heroes we create, we do get caught up in their drama and we can choose whose side we will fall into – a sort of "who's on the Lord's side who" game of chance.

In some cultures, mythology is like the psychic energy that, when taken away or shattered, causes the entire society to collapse as if its very life force rested upon the myth and not the energy of its "myth believing" inhabitants. Myths deal with every aspect of our lives from birth to death and the entire range of human experience including tragedy, joy, love, hate, war, courage, tyranny etc. Our fates are determined by the mythic gods we create and give authority to. Some believe that we cannot exist without myth. It is thought to be our only connection to a spiritual nature no one seems to fully understand and no one can explain. It is the place where gods do what gods do and we as humans fall victim to whatever twists and turns those "doings" take. Myths give us characters, circumstances, events and outcomes and we accept these outcomes as our fate, sensing there is more to it than that, only we can't quite put a finger on what it is that is missing. What is missing is us.

In reality, we live two lives. The first "is" the mythical life. It is the life we want to fit into the world in general. It is the illusory life we are conditioned to view from the very beginning of life on this planet. It is the life of "I" that learns to find a place in the world outside, which is full of other "I's." Some view this as unconsciousness while others view it as consciousness. If we can agree that it is a life that is limited in its awareness of everything else going on around it, is doesn't matter what we call it. Science has proven that conscious awareness or consciousness is extremely limited to the amount of information it can process even though we know the amount of information coming into us is so great as to be overwhelming. The real problem with consciousness is "What should we be conscious of?" This is where the second life plays its part. This is the life of non-consciousness or that part of us that senses a greater reality but is not able to move that awareness into the realm of consciousness. It is what consciousness has identified as the unknown or the unknowable and because it has been identified as such, it puts little or no effort into the understanding of it. We all live these separate lives but the conscious life is so narrow and focused that it blocks out the other life that really has the greater awareness. At times, bits and pieces of it seep through the conscious filters and we glimpse the totality of life we are all a part of, but it is almost always fleeting. Our myths give us context into which we can place these experiences but again, they are only myths and fail to lead us to that inner knowing of self, the second life, that we get glimpses of every now and again.

There is a sort of war between these two lives or sets of awareness. On one hand, our conscious self connects us to the world of which it has identified itself with. That is the world as we see it through our senses and that has been narrowly defined as the realm of our identity. It takes an identity to reconcile something outside that identity into which it can place itself. In other words, I can see the world "out there" and I can place myself in that world. In placing oneself in that world, we develop an identity or self that fits to some degree in that world.

The problem that arises is that when this outer facing identity cannot reconcile the occurrences that come out of our greater awareness, using normal outer world explanations. Maybe it can be viewed as the "mythic" versus the "mystic." It is then that the focus of consciousness zeroes in on this unexplainable awareness and tries to make it fit within its known three dimensional parameters. When it cannot, then the awareness is typically defined as impossible or imaginary. Often it is reconciled to the deep, dark storage banks of the mind never to be considered again. Mythology sometimes eases the frustration of unanswered questions we all have by telling us to have faith that things will be settled in the end. In a way this is true because we all come to an awareness to all meaning sometime in our lives even if it is as we draw our last breath and exit this physical world.

Mythology never fully puts us at ease in its attempts to answer these deeper questions of life or when deep inner awareness meets outward constructs. Mythology requires a certain amount of faith if not absolute blind faith which always tends to leave us feeling cold and alone. Faith is our greatest myth. It is the ultimate shoulder we lean on in those times when deep awareness eludes us. Faith always breaks in the light of greater awareness. We often hear those who have reached profound states of enlightenment claim that just before the new awareness came that they had lost all faith. Faith, then, is a driving force that is the connective glue to our myths but it is always breakable. In other words the failure of faith is what breaks us free of our limiting beliefs. Faith drives us to break free of our myths by forcing us to give up on them!

As all myth is the projection of our inner fears, desires and concerns onto the outer world in which we live, the deeper questions of life, the inner life that is, go unanswered. In our search for answers, we cry out for myth to soothe that which scares us – that which is always left unanswered within. Our outer projections, our myths, require us to believe that somewhere or somehow, out there where we look to non-existent gods, the answers lay. Even our science, which has been very successful at dispelling so many of our myths, looks for the answers to everything "out there" with full faith that someday a theory of everything will finally be developed from which every question can be answered. Science, too, has its own myths!

We, as humans, having accepted so completely the illusion of consciousness, need mythology to help us cope with the unanswered questions of life that loom imposingly over us from time to time throughout our lives. Mythology gives us comfort when unanswerable questions bubble up from a place deep within us that we rarely acknowledge amidst the hustle and bustle of life. We can look to our gods and heroes for explanation and comfort and convince ourselves that they know all and will somehow guide us through whatever it is we question or struggle with. It is a safe way to live a life that, otherwise, seems so mysterious and illusive. Our myths give us place and hope from all that we cannot comprehend in life. Myth is the explanation of illusion we all dwell in and so plays to our conditioning whatever it is. It is the safety we seek from the dark night and it requires faith like conditioning in most cases, since our myths have become so abstract no one who thinks logically could ever accept.

Consider any of our religious traditions, be they Christian, Hindu, Judaism, Muslim, Buddhism or whatever. For some, we are saved from our sins and the impossibility to save ourselves while for others we are saved from oppression and persecution and will be raised and chosen to be above all others. Some will come and go from earth in multiple forms as they struggle over many lifetimes to "get it right" while others who are true to their myth will be exalted in endless bliss and places of glory inconceivable in this three dimensional realm. How could any of these be accepted and internalized without faith? Only an exercise of faith could allow us to believe such things and internalize them in our lives. Faith is the tool ego uses to accept myths that always look outward to something greater than ourselves. Ego asks for faith because ego has never successfully been able to explain God, or answer the questions we all ask about who we are.

The greatest evidence of this is all the religious tenets now existent on earth all contending for exclusive "rightness". Inner knowing, the discovery of God within has no need of faith or myth to explain what the ego wants us to believe. Knowing supersedes faith and dispels all myth. Any search to find the inner self will never lead to faith based conceptions. Faith is always an egoic device and that is why we must never stop searching. As long as we know our foundation is faith based, we cannot accept any conclusion that asks us to believe anything "out there" in the heavens that will eventually provide all the answers. To do so only entombs deeper an inner knowing we all can find. In other words, we replace God with false and fleeting gods. Faith is a necessary part of life and it might even be the key to finding God even though it is a device of the ego to calm the questioning or fearful mind. Faith is the ego's way of expressing that "it" (ego) has no clue.

True faith never stops searching, not even when it grows comfortable with institutional beliefs. When, or if, the search stops, we have given ourselves over to the false gods. As mentioned earlier, we have all heard it said that someone has lost their faith. You can lose faith and ultimately you must lose it to find yourself. Faith motivates us to move forward with belief in some objective but faith can always be lost and often is. Too often, faith is lost because the egoic drive to believe in something abstract becomes untenable to the true self. Perhaps even more often, we simply give up. The cost of believing is too much, so we let go or settle by simply going along with the crowd. Loss of faith takes on many forms, but true replacement of faith can only take the form of knowing and knowing only comes with the discovery of God. Your God. You!

Faith might be thought of as the motivation to fight through the constructs of ego and the illusory life we have come to accept. Faith and myth are necessary elements of the egoic life we live. We all search for basic life meanings, especially since most of those meanings are systematically conditioned out of us from birth. As long as the search of faith continues, we continue to seek out greater awareness and that is good for ultimately finding your true inner self; the god that you are already. There is power in faith, but it is partial power. Full power comes from knowing that you and any mythological God you believe in are one and the same and that you are the only god of your existence and that there are no others before you. The premise of faith is that it asks you to be blind to the unknown and accept outer sources of authority at their word. Knowing asks that your eyes always be opened to the greater awareness we all have within. Know thyself and in so doing, your awareness will comprehend all things. The so-called "theory of everything" will be found in this awareness. It is in this place that our search for myth is no longer necessary as we recognize that we are *the myth*!

Chapter 4

Faith – Our Mythological Partner

Faith is the bedfellow of mythology. But it has woven its way into the very fabric of life we live because while we can never be one hundred percent sure of our beliefs, faith holds us to them, even when they are untrue. It is the paradox of our three dimensional natures to be certain that all things are not possible while having faith that they are. The word faith is sometimes used in conjunction with the words trust and hope. We may find a person hoping to win the lottery and believing with faith unbending that it will happen, only to be disappointed when it doesn't. In extreme cases, some will lose their faith when the events they hoped for did not come to pass. "I'll never trust God again", some will say as their anger and disappointment gets the better of them. Humans are the only living things that have adopted an idea of faith mainly because of our conditioning that something outside of us is greater than us and watches over us in a kind and loving way. Our illusion creates this kind of hope within us and so we look to gods, heroes and others to solve our problems or at least see us through them and even make right in a future time or place.

Faith is like the glue that connects us to outside factors we either see or don't see but believe because that is what we have been taught to believe. Faith is a tool of ego just as caring is. We convince ourselves that whatever our mythological conditioning may be that we will be proven right, our beliefs will prevail over the beliefs of others who are as committed to theirs as we are to our own.

Faith plays into the dual nature of three dimensional life, by locking us into differing positions from others of different conditions and everyone is devoted and fixated on their own position so completely they are contemptuous of any other position. All of our religious wars have been fought over the rigidity of a "faithful" position. Our faith pulls us into positions for which there is no moral basis other than "that is how I was raised or brought up" and we accept these positions solely because someone convinced us it was right and worthy of our conviction. Faith has become the bulwark of many causes but it has also become the cause of much blindness. People believe in things that are inwardly pursued hoping they will be outwardly manifested. There is a common misconception that faith is belief in truth but the truth we find ourselves believing in is likely untrue. It might even be said that most everything we believe or say we know is untrue. As such, faith is really an idea that what is not truth can somehow become truth.

When Jesus spoke of faith, he likened it to a mustard seed. Many have taken his metaphor to mean that very little faith is needed to make big things happen. Jesus was not talking about quantity or even quality of faith, as many believe. In fact, he was not talking about faith at all when he made this comparison. He was describing something other than faith that we must all come to that exceeds faith of any kind. He was talking about knowing or "being" what you are outside of anything else you believe yourself to be. If faith is about anything, it is about inner knowing, but "knowing" supersedes faith.

The mustard seed Jesus described is ultimately a mustard tree. It has all the stuff of a mustard tree even though it is only a seed. In the world of a mustard seed, what is known and only known is that mustard seeds become mustard trees. Mustard seeds do not get wrapped around beliefs that they somehow, perhaps with faith, can become olive trees. Jesus' expression was an admonition to be what you are but in the world of humans, that is a difficult thing to do because we live in a world of egoic reality that "believes" it is something else. Most of us do not accept that we are gods nor do we believe that in any existence can we be anything like God, even though we are gods. It is not enough to simply believe, with faith, that it is so. We must find this awareness and accept that in knowing our "god-ness", we find all that God is, already exists within. We are the seed and all that is god *is* already in the seed! That is our mustard seed. A mustard seed does not wonder what it is or isn't or what it "might" become. It does not believe anything! It simply is.

Perhaps another way for Jesus to have explained this might have been "know you are God, just as the mustard seed knows it is a mustard tree". Therein you find power to overcome anything, to do anything and it costs you nothing. Humans in the illusory state we have created rarely get to see or experience who they truly are in the way a mustard seed does. We are bombarded with so many other things that we are blinded to the greatness of the "tree" within us. The mustard seed has no belief or faith. It simply is, in its purest form, a mustard tree with no illusion and no equivocation. It will do what it does and not wonder about an outcome. Now some will read this and say, "But a mustard seed doesn't have the capability of "thinking" about what it is." This should tell you something about "thinking." Our ability, as humans, to think is what leads us into the quandary of doubting our own make up. We are so caught up in egoic devices that label and define us that we have lost all sight of what we truly are. Jesus metaphor of the mustard seed is precisely about this. In other words, stop "thinking" about what you are or what you are not and simply "be!"

Here is another important point about the idea of knowing. Without attachment to our egoic ideas of what is, we release ourselves from everything that ties us to a faith based reality. Release from any beliefs releases us from anything other than "who" we are. God speaks to us at that point and the only thing we hear is a purity of essence. An essence of what we are. Only in that purity of essence do we discover the great tree within. Therein lies our true power.

Faith is a great device to aid us in finding solace amidst the noise of the world but knowing that we are the seed of God frees us from the noise altogether and allows us to grow into the greatness, the tree, that we truly are. Knowing this requires a complete letting go of everything else in our lives. Everything! Not in the egoic way that says you must give up family, job, friends, etc. and run off to be a monk in Tibet. Release from any idea that anything we have accomplished in life, own, or attach any importance to are of no value to being a "mustard seed." We must "be" gods rather than "hope" to be. Believing is not enough nor is any amount of faith going to change what "might be" from "what is".

We seem to have turned things around in our illusion. We search and train hoping that through our career, our life of goals and beliefs that we will find ourselves and find purpose and meaning to our lives, when, in fact, we find ourselves and discover the seed of God within and that purpose and meaning will take care of themselves. Find God within and you will have the seed of faith, but be the God that you are and you will move mountains.

The seed of faith has no voice. In other words, upon the discovery that each of us is god we rise above the ability of human language to describe what that means. This is "knowing." I refer to this idea of knowing a lot in my writings but I, like so many others, am remiss to be able to articulate in egoic terms, whether religious or scientific, what that means.

No one, who has come to this awareness can. "Knowing," as I refer to it, has nothing to do with the "human" aspect of our existence. It is completely detached from anything physical, which is why science and even basic human logic, have such a difficult time grasping that there is something more to our existence than what we typically see "in front" of our eyes. Yet those who have experienced the "touch" of the divine upon their physical shoulders are never the same. It is as if the awareness they had in front of their eyes is no longer there. Something else deep within holds a vision that is incomprehensible, physically and mentally, and completely overwhelms everything "out there" in the physical world. The vision renders them speechless other than for the, somewhat, vain attempts to use "metaphors" to explain it. The Tao would describe it as "knowing without knowing." In other words spiritual knowing will never be explainable by anything physical.

Faith should never be thought of as "what I want or what I can get." It applies solely to "Who I AM" That is the "works" that is spoken of by Paul the Apostle when he said "faith without works is dead." Uncovering the "who" of your existence is the essence of faith and it requires work to do it because all our lives we have been told that not only can we not move mountains but we are not worthy of the highest glory we give our gods. Our faith is a vehicle that can carry us only so far but our works must continue to unmask the identities we have surrounded ourselves with. It is in this unmasking that we draw nearer to what it is we are and it is in that knowing that mountains are moved. We are the "tree" not the "seed." The seed does not give life to the tree. The tree is always the tree and the seed knows this. "Being the seed is being the tree."

Many Christian scholars have expanded the meaning of this metaphor with ideas of "what do we do to make the seed grow?" Obviously we respond with things like plant it and water it and fertilize it and care for it and it requires these things to have it become the tree. Somehow in these various "broadened" analogies we compare these "works" of planting, fertilizing, etc. to the works we are told will, likewise, nourish us and have the object of our faith realized but none of this matters if the seed we are trying to sow is different from our true seed. In other words you cannot *become* God. Why? Because you already are God!

Faith might be better viewed as something that drives us to a point of breaking ourselves from the hold of physical reality upon us. It drives us to give up on our ideas of truth and simply give ourselves over to other forces, as we might refer to them. Many, after breaking will create new stories that include the ideas from before and maintain a new view of themselves that include the gods and hero's they believed in only now the story is altered somewhat. Faith at this point is now formed around a new story or new untruth. The pull of our conditioning almost always sneaks back into our mental picture of this new reality that we, again, must be broken of. All our lifetime of conditioned knowledge and egoic structure must be broken so that any idea of truth whatsoever is no longer held. We are literally freed from all ideas of knowledge and truth.

Faith is not about holding on to beliefs and ideas we think to be true or important. It is ultimately about letting go of everything we believe about our physical experience. *Faith is letting go!* It is never about holding on and regardless of what we place our faith in no part of it will ever be the truth we seek. The truth we seek is already within us and it requires no other effort than to find that inner awareness of who we are outside our physical natures. Faith is not believing in what is true, rather it is not believing anything we think we know at all. It is freeing ourselves from beliefs altogether and letting the essence of who we are, gods, become our awareness. This form of awareness cannot be explained. It can only be known and it is unshakeable in any reality.

Faith hooks us to our beliefs and our beliefs are the result of our particular conditioning which make them more fantasy then fact. In the light of "knowing" faith fades quickly and all desire to "know" in human terms ceases to be important anymore. Faith is acceptance that the mystery of the tree is no more important than the mystery of the seed. All that is important is the "knowing" that is without human description and physical form. True faith is a release from that which we have believed to accepting that outside of our beliefs there really exists the unbelievable!

Chapter 5

Emotions; Trees and Human Bark

A significant part of our existence, our reality, consists of the emotional states we switch from throughout the course of our day and these states subsequently give texture and form to the experience of living. We identify others as their emotional state and sometimes in describing them, we will reference such states. For instance, we might describe someone as moody, happy, full of life, vibrant, sad, depressed, angry, mean, kind, caring, fearful, and others.

Emotions are taught to us and when we recount our own lives or watch young parents raise their children, we see this teaching of emotional states. We might recall our own parents describing a situation, perhaps someone falls ill or dies, and we are told that we should be sad and feel remorse. As children, we don't fully understand these terms but as we watch other adults play out their emotions in various situations, we learn to feel sadness, anger, happiness, joy or whatever emotional reaction a given situation elicits.

Our conditioning includes the connection to events occurring in three dimensional reality and their subsequent transition into emotional states. Emotions become the strongest part of our egos in that they can rarely be dealt with in rational terms. In other words, it is much harder to change what we feel emotionally than what we know intellectually. Sometimes knowing is connected to feelings (emotions) and the ability to change is even greater. It is true that feeling is exhilarating and at times our physical bodies tingle all over with goose bumps or the hair on the back of our necks stands on end.

Events and situations that cause emotional states in us are long remembered and deeply impressed upon by our psyche and these impressions become our view of reality. It is as if the cells of our bodies, our biology as it were, holds the memory of the original experience. It is literally etched into us. We all know such times in our lives when things happened that left what we call an emotional impression on us and the recollection of such events always brings with it our emotional state at that time. Emotions as a part of our existence are a great gift of three dimensional reality. They allow us to feel a state of awareness brought about by the physical reaction we have to any given experience. We learn these states and the reactions we're supposed to have to them. Throughout the course of our lives, as experience is added upon, so too our emotional states are added upon and reinforced.

Emotions can be generally categorized as that which makes us joyful or happy and that which makes us sad or unhappy. Happy and sad creates the basic duality we find in our existence and the major creator of most conflicts. The events of our lives and their subsequent emotional states fall, in varying degrees, into one of these states. As children, we did not know such emotional states. We came to know, through conditioning, that certain acts we engaged in were met with disapproval (unhappiness) or approval (happiness) which over time have been locked into our minds and bodies in such a way that the emotional states have become a part of the way we view and respond to life. On the extreme side, as young children we may have experienced abuse or neglect by adults more powerful than us and whom we could not challenge or rebut. In such cases we develop strong emotional states such as fear, anger or frustration and because of the circumstances in which these states developed it is often impossible to ever know how they came to be. At a pre-language age the intellectual ability to articulate such emotional states did not exist and so we simply have the emotions without the explanation for them. Often these are never reconciled even as mature, well-adjusted adults. Most emotions run deep and are very personal to the point of being painful physically.

The duality at play with our various sad, happy states puts us in the realm of judging life events, emotionally, as good or bad and based on our particular conditioning that elicited those states. It puts our life on one side or another of something that is totally ego made. In fact, when you consider the age at which most of our emotional states developed we were far too young and immature to reason in any way what was going on that caused the state in the first place. At such an age we are highly susceptible to those we look to for protection and security and they, having been conditioned much the same have no other way but to share what they were led to believe and emotionally feel. It is difficult to break out of a cycle when you don't have the faintest idea that you are even in a cycle. Thus, children learn emotional states that play on the side of happy or sad depending on the circumstances they are shown and life becomes the ordeal of "sides" that we spend our lives being on this one or the other. Ego is the great divider.

One of the best ways to know how ego works in your life is to observe how much passion is involved in a particular issue you find yourself connected to. If there are two sides to an issue, and there always are in a duality, and you are passionately devoted to one or the other, ego has a tight grip on your life. Emotionality is the egoic way to make us believe that our cause or purpose is important. Passion is often looked at as something we must have when pursuing our dreams. It, too, is referred to when someone has enacted what we might refer to as great evil, e.g. "crimes of passion. Passion gives us a sense of gravity and importance for our various causes. It is our greatest display of caring which has become a noble act. This is how we come to care.

Children are not born caring. They are taught to care and what to care about. Children are actually born with *will* which is the motivation of the gods. Will is action. It is not passion or caring and you see this in children as they grow from infancy up to the ages of seven or eight. They are infinitely curious and completely without fear of any kind. They don't know fear. How could they? Fear takes training and conditioning like all other emotions. In fact, fear has become a widely used and accepted training tool to teach the duality of life which adds complication to our own navigation of it. "Others can hurt you..., fear for your life." "Don't do that or you'll be punished." Everywhere we hear fear being used as a means to condition others to do, or not do, something we believe to be wrong or right.

We also see the converse of this as well in that people will use rewards and accolades to condition us to move a certain direction. "Do this and you'll be rewarded." Guilt, which is another form of fear, is one of the ego's greatest tools to get us to accept the condition of our, so called, reality. All the emotional states we know get intertwined into a web of life that distorts and confuses the innate awareness we all possess. We confuse reality with our conditioning and say things and ask of others to follow our reasoning based on years of "getting to" the way we are.

We attach the greatest of our meaningful words to our emotions and use them as tools to control and manipulate others around us. The conditional word "if" has become one of our great guilt devices when it is attached to a statement designed to initiate guilt in us. For instance, you may hear someone say "If you respect me, you will not talk to me that way," or perhaps one of the most widely used by teenagers, especially boys, "If you love me, you'll let me." We all know what it feels like to feel guilt, sadness, joy, happiness and all the other emotional states we ascribe to the human family, but we never seem to ask where they came from. In fact, we have institutionalized all forms of emotions and created barriers around them that make them further unbreakable shackles around the situations and circumstances of our lives.

Most of us feel life through these emotional shackles and we all tend to teeter-totter between the various ups and downs we experience emotionally and these states become tightly fused to the individual we become over time. In essence, life is one big emotional experience. We look for balance, but have difficulty finding it because something opposite of what we wanted appears in our reality becoming the next "thing" in a continuous cycle of going from the state of happiness to unhappiness. With all the emotional conditioning we come to accept as reality, we begin using familiar platitudes such as "That's life" or "That's the hand I was dealt", etc. to placate our particular state.

There is much being said in the world today that we attract what we think about. We are told to think of only good things, such as abundance, good relationships, successful job or career, bigger home or car, kids that mind, non-meddling in-laws, and any number of other things we have determined will make us individually and collectively happy. We are told to think about only those things that will make us happy and by so doing we will attract them to us. We are also told that if we "feel" for things with deep emotion, even passion, they will manifest sooner as emotions engage the universe, we are told, to a much larger degree.

Who doesn't want only the biggest and best things in life, e.g. the things we have been conditioned to believe are important such as careers, homes, wealth, happy and fun relationships, mental and physical health, spiritual understanding etc.? So important have these things become in our reality that all of our identity is wrapped up in achieving them. Such has become the measure of success. Even those who would profess to help us achieve such things will use the emotions of fear and guilt to have us use their particular techniques for gaining all the things we have come to define success or a happy life as.

How often do we hear from them a confirmation of "bad economic times" in order to drive home the message that we need what they have? Fear the times "out there" but "Oh wait, I can help you!" We all tend to condition our assertions with the preface of what's wrong with something before inserting our particular viewpoint as the solution! Here's a truth: *there are no unsuccessful lives!* In human terms only, the odds of any one of us being here at this time and in our own unique place and circumstances is so remote as to defy all statistical laws. Your being here is one of the greatest miracles to have ever occurred and couldn't possibly be considered anything but successful! Even knowing this the ego wants something more to be convinced so we must spend our lives struggling to achieve something it knows will never happen and ultimately sends us into fits of emotional despair.

The egoic mind will never be able to comprehend a life without emotion. It is simply too wrapped up in the idea that emotion is what gives life feeling, richness and passion. In fact we are often told that our emotions can be a good barometer of whether our focus and intentions are good or bad. "If it feels good, do it" we are told.

How about that? I love to eat rich, sweet and gooey foods that are fattening and if used excessively, unhealthy. But I love the sensation of taste and exhilaration I feel when I eat such foods. It truly does "feel good!" I love to drink sugary soft drinks, and to eat salty snacks and treats and nothing could be finer then a Snickers bar and a Coca Cola! I love doing only certain things at my job so I will only do those things from now on. I hate cooking for my children so I will no longer do it since it does not make me feel good. I hate school but love sex. Gambling gives me a euphoric high as do various drugs. "Do that" we are told because those things make us happy and we don't want the downside of happiness to play out in anyway in our lives. Make more money because money will set you free to do more of the things you believe make you happy such as travel, fine dining, more recreation, more things, etc. Nothing could be more absurd than using the emotional sense of feeling good as a barometer for what we pursue and experience in life!

We are also told that the stronger we feel about something the more quickly it will show up in our experience. "Get emotional about your wants and desires." This, we are told, is the way to "align" our minds to the things we need to have in our lives in order to be happy, successful and ultimately fulfilled. This, however, is the essence of illusion because when we are in these emotional states we become convinced that something greater and more magnificent is just a little ways off, out there, waiting for us to set our focus on and achieve. So too are the negatives we experience. All these things play into the idea that out there somewhere is a solution to our various emotional states and that our focus on whatever it is, is the way to either enhance or overcome a particular state. This is exactly what ego wants us to believe. This is the illusion we are in and as long as we accept that life comes to us from out there somewhere in the universe we will never regain control of a non-illusory life. Our emotions tie us directly to what we think is real and the current thinking is that we are choosing between positive outcomes over negatives ones because we can emotionally control events outside ourselves.

This is how we are told the law of attraction works but what we are not told is that we do not have to live a life predicated on the choices we must make. The mind is the sole creator of the duality we experience when, in fact, we do not have to make choices. We can replace choice with knowing. That is, the intuitive knowing we all possess if we but learn to hear our own inner voice that is completely detached from anything physical. We have all heard this voice and know it, if we let ourselves remember what it was like as a child when we walked the earth without fear or any idea that we were not the creative center of the universe. We all knew this at one time, and experienced life in a way we cannot fathom as adults. Infant children have no concept of choice until we teach it to them. Infant children are without emotion until we show them, through our own responses to the "choices" we have been conditioned to identify and respond to.

Every one of us learns and eventually teaches what we have learned to others in our experience and we teach in a very absolute way. We even say things like "I don't want my children to go through some of the experiences I had. We want those we teach to avoid what we identify as our own mistakes or trials, not considering that what we are teaching them is what was taught to us. Coupled with specific teachings we are also taught how to feel about a particular situation. By observation of others close to us, who exhibit their emotional responses to life's twists and turns we in turn learn how to emotionally respond to our own set of life's twists and turns. It might be said that the only way we hurt our children is by teaching them what we believe and how to feel about those beliefs. In other words, our slants, slants them! We condition out of them what was conditioned out of us and we do it unknowingly.

We like to say "We choose our life based on our values." We like to believe that our values are what we are at our core, even though we are born into this world without any earthly values. Again, values are something we are taught and our so-called values are a reflection of those who taught us theirs. We are born gods with nothing but light and inner knowing that exceeds all the knowledge man has acquired to this point. We are conditioned to be human with earthly values and are expected to acquire emotional states which attach us to the outer world. We have come to believe that the way we see is "what is."

There is nothing wrong with finding or having happiness in our lives, but the nature of life as we have come to accept it calls for opposition in all things. This means that with the happiness we seek comes the unhappiness also. Many new age teachers and self-help gurus will tell us this is necessary for contrasts so that we know the difference between the two. This idea is not so in the spiritual form. Being spiritual means that every aspect of life experience is there to enjoy and embrace in every way possible. Life is sweet. No part of it is "not sweet" to the god within us. This is why we are here and just being here in physical form is our only purpose.

None of our emotional states have any meaning other than, we, as gods, having this incredible human experience, get to experience all the things our humanness allows us to experience. We are already greater than any of the conditions or circumstances we experience here on earth and we cannot fail in the experience! As part of our conditioning we talk a lot about success and failure but the fundamental aspect of human experience is that we cannot fail at life. Our existence is so much more than the experience of our unique humanness. Regardless of our choices there is no wrong or right. There simply is no choice that can alter the essence of what you are nor can it alter the experience you will have as a god living in a human body. Life sings; it always sings, in spite of how we feel about it or the choices we make, as humans, or what parts of it we like or dislike. Life is always honest and sings in spite of our emotional conditioning or judgments of it.

Siddhartha, who would become the first Buddha, began his spiritual life searching for the reasons for all the suffering in the world. It perplexed him and while he became enlightened, he never saw an end to suffering, violence and calamity. He even experienced great loss when his own family and childhood home was captured and destroyed by warring factions. He experienced everything life offered including physical ailments and old age. However, when he was old and coming to his own end, he told his closest followers, "Life is so very sweet." He never saw an end to suffering and violence or any of the things he sought to understand when he began his journey. He only saw the "sweetness" of it all and his life was complete. He died in peace, even though his dying may have been caused by diseased food. None of it mattered. Life, all of life, was sweet, for Buddha, but so too can it be for us, if we let go of our emotional judgments of it.

The author Haruki Murakami is often quoted with his observation that "Pain is inevitable. Suffering is optional," The mind creates suffering out of the false notion that "pain" need not be existent in our experience. It is craziness to think we can go through life without everything that it encompasses which includes pain. The unique ability of the mind, however, is to create a drama, a story that paints the walk through life as treacherous, dangerous or, sometimes, unexciting. All suffering resides in the mind! So does happiness!

Our emotions can be thought of as a thick shell that forms around us which protects us from the onslaughts of those things we believe can hurt us or the way to let in and embrace those things we believe bring pleasure. Emotions are the feedback of ego that either harden or soften with life experience. We are literally wrapped in our emotions and our bodies have been conditioned to reflect the sensations we have equated with certain experience throughout our lives. For most our emotions harden us to the things we believe are harmful to us and in the process of hardening we lose our sensitivity to the wonders that surround us.

Growing up in the Pacific Northwest, I have always had a certain affinity to trees. Washington State is referred to as the Evergreen state and it was difficult to go anywhere without having a sense of being surrounded by trees of every kind, but most of all, evergreens. As a boy, I loved walking in pine scented forests on warm summer days and smelling the richness of the soil mingled with the bark of various trees, shrubs and undergrowth. I remember thinking, as I wandered about those thick, forested areas that I could actually hear the smells. It was as if all the various scents of everything living gave off a noise or vibration that my ears could hear. And yet, it wasn't my ears that heard it. It was something deeper and more mysterious that I could not identify. It was as if my entire body vibrated at the same frequency of this buzz and mingling of so many life forms. The colors filled me with more than visual stimulation. I could hear them too.

Everything was alive but not in the ordinary sense that things live. There was a buzz to all of it that affected something else inside of me other than my physical senses. I was simply alive with an illumination and everything was a part of it. It was the dance of the living and I was caught up in it in such a way that it filled me with wonderment and awe. To be so tuned into the brilliance and loudness surrounding me, to this day, is one of the greatest experiences of my life and rarely do I feel the closeness to life I felt then.

It seemed then that the trees knew me and while amongst them, I knew them as well. I cared for them, then, as I do now. I sensed them in a way that I could almost hear them speak to me and each time this happened, I knew of their gentleness and their great connection to earth and sky. I often found myself, sitting in the cool shade they provided, wondering what it was like to reach for the sky as they did and how beautiful it must be to see the things they saw. I would also wonder what the part of them I could not see, the roots, experienced. There was as much of them in the earth as above it. I knew the trees knew the earth in a way I could not possibly know and so I asked them what it was like to know the world above and below at the same time. They answered that knowing what they know could only come from being as they are – still, quiet, strong and ever sensitive to the heartbeat of life. They always listen quietly, but steadfastly, for the sounds of every living thing. Their roots reached deeply into the earth and could feel her heartbeat tapping out a rhythmic song that soothed all who could hear it.

They told me I could hear the earth's heartbeat if I listened and was very quiet. I would press my ear against the tree and while I could not hear a rhythmic beat as they described it, I felt the warmth of the bark against my face. It was the same warmth I felt when I laid my head on my mother's lap. It was comforting warmth that penetrated my soul and I found myself sensing their life more vividly than any human. It never occurred to me that the trees I loved to be amongst were not as alive and aware as I or anyone else. I sensed their connection to the earth and air.

Like sentinels, always watching within and without. At that time, I knew nothing about the dimensionality of existence. I only marveled that the ability of trees to see into the earth and into the heavens must give them an awareness of life on earth as no other. I appreciated their tenderness toward me. They gave me shelter from the rain, shade from the sun and always security. I felt safe when with them.

I don't know the science or biology of tress. I think everyone believes they are living; however, it is not likely that science would accept that trees are conscious and aware, like humans. Conscious awareness is a product of the brain, they would tell us, and trees do not have brains. Perhaps the greatest act of the arrogance of man is to consider himself the highest of all life forms on earth. It is an egotistical view of life to think that consciousness resides only in humans and to a lesser degree that humans can judge the intelligence of so-called lesser life forms. We know that all things, whether we consider them animate or inanimate, live. Life is a vibration, a dance of particles so small that science, with all its sophisticated instrumentation, cannot detect.

We are a part of that dance that everything is a participant in. Everything on this planet, in the universe, is alive and conscious of its own dance and if we put aside the idea that, because of our brain we somehow know better, we too can experience the vibration. We participate in the vibration whether we sense it or not. Only the ego steers us away from that knowing. Odd that while all things dance to life, man, the so-called highest of all life forms on earth, has created a device that shields him from the dance that everything else in life experiences. That device is our emotions which harden with the onslaught of life experiences or soften when we perceive that experience is nonthreatening. It need not be that way, but we have let our ego create in us a self-importance that is only recognizable by other self-important egos.

When I was amongst the trees of the forest, I never felt the judgment I constantly felt among my fellow humans. I knew no shame or embarrassment and always had a rich sense of who I was at a deeply inner level that I could easily access in their presence. I wore no masks and had I done so the trees would have seen through it. As I have grown older, the strong feelings I have when among trees continues. I feel a sense of deep reverence and I am comforted in their presence. I still talk to them and they to me, although they seem more guarded than when I was a child. I think perhaps they are not as trusting of adult humans as they are of children because adult humans have not proved to be the best stewards of all things animate or inanimate. I wonder.

When I think about trees and humans now, I am struck by the definition we might give to each when we compare them. The tree, we might say, is strong, rigid, and immovable, while the human is fragile, vulnerable, and flexible. Emotionally speaking, however, the opposite is more likely the case. Unlike the tree, the ego of man has become strong, rigid and immovable; emotionally bound to thoughts and fears. The tree, like man, has a shell around it — its bark.

The bark of the tree is soft compared to the inner surface which the bark protects. However, it is the bark that is exposed to the world in which the tree stands. The bark feels the cold blast from a northern wind or the heat of a sun drenched summer day. It takes the rain in spring and the snows of winter. All that Mother Nature throws at the tree is absorbed by the bark that always stays soft relative to the inner tree. Humans, on the other hand, whose bark is the ego, become rigid, and inflexible when subjected to the barbs of life inflicted by other humans or natural circumstances. Instead of remaining soft and flexible to life, as the tree, humans build defenses and barriers that shut out anything that has caused pain, suffering and sorrow. The tree, on the other hand, is always open to life. Every aspect of it! Regardless of the perils it faces, it stands tall and erect, impeccable, living life to the very end without any hardening whatsoever toward those things it naturally faces in life.

Ego becomes so emotionally hardened that any sense of inner strength is vanquished and life becomes limited and a struggle to avoid those circumstances which caused it to harden itself originally. Ego does not live life; it avoids it. The bark of a tree embraces life in every way remaining soft, flexible and open to everything that comes its way.

We could all learn a great deal from trees and other living things. Other living things accept life in all its forms and, rather than fight against, they live with it, accepting all that life offers and basking in the light of each new day. Regardless of what each day brings, we should embrace it and revel in each spectacular moment it provides. Like my friends the trees, our bark, our egos, our emotions should weather the storms of life and never harden against it. Like the trees we should stand strong and tall, absorbing all that life brings to us and not stand against it.

As a boy and now as a man, I've always known trees to be gentle of spirit, but strong, and powerful and yet with all that strength, they stood quiet, majestic and strong. Even when the wind blows and catches their branches, they bend and sway gracefully, accepting everything about the experience they have. When the wind blows, they remain calm and gracefully move with it. They adjust to it calmly and quietly. I used to lay on my back looking up through the branches and watch them move gently in the wind and marvel at how flexible, how accepting of everything they were. It made me smile as I watched them live with ease and grace. Those were magical times and even now, I can detect an aura about them not unlike that of humans. The auras of trees, however, are always pure without any distortions; they lose no energy to life, like we humans do. Trees move gracefully with life while humans find reasons to move against it; fight it and question why.

Bark is to trees what emotions are to humans. Like bark our emotions should not become resistant to the surroundings or circumstances we find ourselves in. Instead of letting our minds create barriers to life and hardening ourselves to the rich and complex circumstances we encounter, like the bark of trees, we need to gracefully move with everything we experience and accept everything that touches us along the way.

Otherwise we miss the splendor of experience that human existence offers. I am often surprised by gurus and others who make statements about individuals who no longer serve them and that they must cut them loose from their circle of acquaintances. What a loss! "You no longer serve me!" What about our service to them? This is a hardening. Our view of life and everything that happens in our particular experience need not ever be reason to harden ourselves against it.

Emotions are the sensory conversion of physical experience into spiritual awareness. The softer they become the more of that experience we enjoy and the more expansive it becomes. If we can find a way to recognize that our emotions are an aspect of the human experience that need not become the predicate of that experience we can begin to open ourselves to a far grander sensory experience. Even those things that we find distasteful about our human experience can be gems that brighten our lives and add variety, richness and enjoyment. We owe to ourselves to be open to such vastness of experience.

Chapter 5

Cosmic Deception

In early 1980, after I had worked and scratched my way from an inspector to various levels in a quality organization, I was allowed to take a position as a quality manager for a small company located in my home town. It would be the beginning of a long career of managing quality and operations organizations for many companies I would work for in the future. In that first managerial position, I was given a book by a great man and mentor titled The New Managerial Grid by Blake and Mouton. I eagerly read the book as I was determined to be the best manager I could be. Without prior experience or a college education, I was determined to keep up with new ideas and concepts that would help me stay up with, or ahead of, those who were better educated. Reading that book would give me my very first exposure to the "Maslow Hierarchy of Needs" as they applied to workers in a typical workplace. I was fascinated by the simplicity of the hierarchy that placed basic needs, such as food, shelter, water, etc. at the base of the pyramid and the higher form of "self-actualization" at the top. In between the bottom and top levels, there were other levels which all built upon the other lower ones and allowed greater opportunities for fulfillment in life, developmental growth, and ultimately, the discovery of inner self.

As I moved through my career keeping this managerial model always in mind, I was always curious about the lack of self-actualized people I found at my level and those above me. It seemed that as I observed those who reached levels of attainment and comfort described by the hierarchy, the fewer "self-actualized" individuals there were. What I did find was what appeared to be a higher determination to achieve even more of the things they felt were important and essential to life. Even those who reached a place where the rest of the world would say they were highly successful seemed to be unsatisfied and wanting more.

    I would marvel at some of the descriptions these so-called successful people would come up with to define what it was they needed to feel successful or happy themselves. It always boiled down to more and the "more" was just more grandiose versions of the same things they had already attained. As I had accepted this reality, I was sure that all of these others had simply misunderstood the concepts of the hierarchy of needs and that somehow I got it. I reasoned that when I attained financial stability and had attained all the things at the lower levels of the pyramid, I would surely "actualize" and my soul would surely stand on holy ground. I knew I would be the one to realize my spiritual nature and find the place within that would open me up to a pinnacle of mental, physical, emotional and spiritual well-being.

    It never happened. It seems the further I went up the pyramid, the further away self-actualization would get. My problems, that were supposed to be going away, only seemed to get bigger and more complex with the passing of time. I reached a place where I could travel, purchase things I previously could not afford, etc. I had money to retire on and sufficient for my needs. There was also recognition in my job for outstanding work and enthusiasm and I was a "go to" individual when things needed to get done. I was physically healthy; I had presence and was considered a leader by my peers, subordinates and superiors. I had a wonderful family. I was able to provide just about anything they wanted that would enrich and enhance their lives and I was a proud father and husband. Why, then, was this idea of self-actualization so fleeting? I never seemed to be able to get a hold of it, even though I met the requirements of the hierarchy of needs. My spirit was never at rest. In fact, it seemed to be worse than when I was scraping by. What was I missing and why was it that so many others I observed seemed to be no closer either?

This would bother me for thirty years. Then one day, I was reading from the works of Carlos Castaneda's <u>Teachings of don Juan</u> series of books, where he recounted the story of himself lamenting to don Juan about the poor, hapless state of some little boys cleaning the scraps of food from the tables of a little restaurant Carlos was observing. In the conversation that followed with don Juan, Carlos explained how sad it was for those boys. He even exclaimed to don Juan his great concern for his fellow men and that the world of those little boys was "ugly and cheap". This raised the ire of don Juan and he asked Carlos, "You think you are better off, don't you?" Carlos replied that he did and explained that "In comparison to those children's world, mine is infinitely more varied and rich in experience and in opportunities for personal satisfaction and development." Don Juan laughed at Carlos for this, explaining that Carlos had no way of knowing what kind of opportunities existed for those boys.

The real crux of the story continues as don Juan establishes that being a "man of knowledge" is the highest achievement for a human. A "man of knowledge" might be don Juan's way of describing a "self-actualized" individual. In any case, don Juan asked Carlos if anything he has done with any of his experience, opportunities or freedoms could help him become a "man of knowledge". Carlos answered no, and don Juan asked, "Then how could you feel sorry for those children?"

I observed a similar thing while working with my Sister in a village in Honduras where she had bought property and had set up a small clinic for the people of that village and surrounding areas. There was every form of disease and malnutrition and every single person who came to her clinic would receive a dose of a de-worming medicine just for showing up. Parasites infested everyone because there was no infrastructure anywhere in Honduras that could provide basic needs as described above.

Dirt floors and stick huts packed with mud were common and trips to the river were where the villagers drank, washed clothing and dishes and bathed themselves. One day my sister and I were talking about the children who always seemed to be hanging around. I observed that they all seemed so happy and asked my sister if she thought these little ones stood a chance of ever having a spiritual awareness. She exclaimed immediately that it was not possible in the least as they were struggling with so many other issues that to discover their own divine nature would be impossible. I was surprised by her response and asked, "How do you explain that they all seem so happy?" Her response was just as immediate and similarly direct. "I don't know" she said, "it puzzles me too because they have nothing and they have nothing to look forward to!"

I was not satisfied with this answer and pressed her a bit further on the subject of spirituality. She insisted that "basic needs" had to be served before anyone could advance to a more "enlightened" state and that outside the work she was doing to help the little ones in her village few if any had any chance of having anything other than a life of poverty and disease. I remember being saddened by her assessment of those children and pondered the sweetness in their faces and their complete exhilaration with the life they were living. Not once did I ever hear a child complain of their circumstances and everywhere I saw gratitude and acceptance, happiness and joy. In fact, when I was getting ready to leave three of the young children wrote me letters in Spanish thanking me for coming to visit them and expressing how much they loved having me there with them. What moved me most; however, were their wishes for me. Each of these wonderful children wished for me to have "everything I desired" in life and to be happy. Without having any concept of how "good" I had things in my life, how abundant and full of the things that are supposed to help us become "actualized," these children were completely giving of themselves. What they gave was more than all the riches in the world.

They gave their love, their friendship and from the very depths of their souls they spoke to mine. They were without labels or identifiers. They knew nothing of their "lack" which was a label I, my sister and others had put on them. They were living life "sweetly" without any hold to an image others thought they should wear. Their "giving" to me was from the depths of someone deeply spiritual but without, even, the label of "spirituality."

They were divine and it didn't matter if they knew what that meant or not. Life for them was a treat as was my life when I was with them. I wept when I read the words of giving and concern for my happiness. Spiritually speaking these were the great ones. Amidst, the squalor, disease and rampant poverty, as we in the west would define it; I witnessed majesty as I have never seen it. I stood among giants and I trembled before them. I could no longer feel any sorrow for these children as my sorrow for them turned to sorrow for myself. I had become the judge of their existence and what I had seen for them was destroyed by what they already knew about existence. In desolation they knew more than I ever hoped to. They were humble; I was embarrassed. I was completely undressed by the "gods" of this tiny little village and I have never been the same since. My prayer since that visit has been that the children of this village never discover the labels we put on them and that their simple view of life never gives way to the noise of our, so called, "actualized" descriptions.

The "Hierarchy of Needs" is inverted. Surely spiritual awareness, which I had sought for so many years, is not a property of attainment, acclaim, and fulfillment of so-called basic needs. Spiritual awareness, self-actualization, or whatever you choose to call it is our very *first* aspect; it is the very core of our divine nature. How true the New Age statement that "we are spiritual beings having a human experience". There is nothing we must attain to in order to achieve spiritual awakening. In fact, it might be considered an arrogant assumption that we must somehow become something we are not, nor may ever be, in order to achieve higher states of awareness. One might ask, "What chance does the poor and infirm have of ever reaching higher states of awareness if they must rise above basic needs when such a possibility may never present itself in their lifetimes?" We all sense a kind of hypocrisy at such a question because we know that some of our greatest spiritual icons came from such circumstances. Some even went from incredible wealth and royalty to a life of poverty and begging as a way to find the awareness I was convinced must come some other way.

We are spiritual beings. Our first state of existence is a spiritual one and it is the human-ness of our earthly existence that conditions us to think that the human is not the *second* state but the first. The focal point of our existence, the peak of the pyramid, if you will, is our most basic knowing, and poverty and lack is equally able as is wealth and riches, or education and intellect, to drive us from or to that knowing. Even health is sometimes equated to a good spiritual life and yet we see so many who are sickly, even bed-ridden and near death who have clarity of life and a sweetness that can only come from a divine knowing and awareness.

Each of us, regardless of our own condition, is totally free. We can change ourselves in the blink of an eye and there is nothing in this life that can take that from us. Each of us is spiritual beyond our wildest imaginings. Gods we are, and gods we will always be. The so-called conditions we say or think prevent us from knowing are illusions of the mind-created reality which we accept as our nature. Nothing we possess or accomplish or attain in this physical reality will ever come close to our true value as divine beings who are crowned with glory from before time. Nothing in this life matters more than the rediscovery of that knowing which each of us possess as infinite beings. This is why it is so critical to learn how to quiet the mind from its endless chatter. The chatter upholds what the mind thinks we are, and consequently, we reinforce that over and over and over.

Ultimately, there is no hierarchy of needs. There is no a hierarchy at all. There is only "being". For most of us, that means finding the seeker, not the sought. The sought is ever present. The part of us that seeks must think about that which it seeks in order to know it when it finds it. The problem is that thinking is incapable of defining that which is sought and so will never find it. This is why we must stop seeking. Seeking equals thinking and thinking is to the sought as the clouds are to the sun. We know the sun is there, we just can't see it. What we are and have always been is ever present. It is only obscured by the clouds hovering over it. Clouds of thinking and chattering.

There is no circumstance or condition that precludes anyone from remembering their own divine nature. No attainment in physical life can assure us of an opportunity, greater or lesser, to find the God of our own nature and to reach a state of awareness that fully comprehends the unknown. We already know the answers to all of the questions. They lie within each of us and the discovery of them is a personal journey that only we as individuals can take. No teachers or guides are needed for this personal inner quest. Only quiet. In stillness, we know God; we know ourselves.

We can seek out guides, mentors and gurus to help us and give pointers but each of us, at some point, will be required to stand on our own and pass through the "refiners fire" alone. After passing through, we will know that the greatest part of our existence as humans has only been a shell. We will realize the power of our own spiritual nature and the physical aspect of us was nothing more than a vehicle to walk us through a human experience and that all of our identity with physical things is nothing compared to our unique and divine natures. The divine nature of man is found in every walk of life, in every condition, and every culture. There are no exclusions and the diversity of experience through the ages is testament that each of us can find our own unique path to God. Every minute of our lives doing whatever it is we do is the pathway to that discovery of self that knows the divine is within. Every turn, every climb, every twist of fate is the spiritual knocking on the door of the physical. All we must do is silence the mind and listen to the stillness.

There are no heroes outside what we are and when we decide to see that in ourselves is when we begin to understand that the greatness of life only exists because of "our own" greatness.

Chapter 6

What's Happening?

There is a greeting westerners have used for many years upon seeing each other that simply goes, "what's happening"? There was a television sitcom with the title "What's Happening" back in the 1970s as well. That query, as to what's happening, has in many ways become a greeting of sorts or an expression of good will at the meeting of friends or acquaintances. It has become a part of our language that asks others to look forward or backward and describe what has happened and what will be happening.

It is the nature of our mind created reality to steer our awareness away from the now that, in truth, is the only thing happening and, onto what is not happening. Most of us, in fact, are conditioned to never look at what is happening right now and so our lives begin to look like narratives of things past or future. They literally become what is not happening even though we like to believe that this not happening is what is really happening.

We see this not happening in every aspect of life. We are told from the very beginning of our lives to get this or that or be this or that. We are stood against examples of the things we are instructed to get or be and told this is how it should be. We are reminded that in our getting or being that that's when it will happen for us. While we are never told what "it" is the admonition to get it is forceful and persuasive. Most of us learn well and get caught up in the conditioning, reinforcing it for others and teaching it anew to our children. Rarely do we ever look at the reason the way we are is because we are taught to be that way.

Nor do we ask why we were taught to be that way and who taught our teachers to be the way they are. Most of us merely perpetuate what has been going on for generations, and what has been going on for generations is the minds version of what's happening.

The minds version of what is happening is, in fact, what's not happening? Consider the things we think about or talk to ourselves about on a regular basis. Most of our minds are talking without any conscious awareness of the conversation going on in our heads and the majority of that conversation has nothing, whatever to do with what's happening.

When I was working full time I would often think about what I would tell my boss about a certain situation or how I would run the company or department if I were in his or her shoes. I would create elaborate arguments and rehearse them over and over so if the situation presented itself I would be all ready to go. Sometimes I would talk out loud with others telling them what I planned to say or do if the right opportunity would appear. Typically, when situations or opportunities did appear for me to direct the conversation I had so carefully planned they didn't go anything at all like I thought they would. I would leave wondering what that was all about and I would find myself rehearsing what I should have said or could have said. Again, more unconscious conversation in my mind trying to resolve what's not happening. If I wasn't looking at the future I was looking at the aftermath of the past. My mind never stopped these discussions. It stressed me out.

Other things I would worry about were the stability of the company and about what I was sure would be layoffs or cutbacks that would not only affect me but many others as well. Again, my mind would begin to consider alternatives or solutions for events that had not happened and may or may not happen. I would stress out over these mind created scenarios and wonder and talk to myself, sometimes to a point of exhaustion. We all do this to some degree or another. We talk to ourselves about the spouse or children, schools, vacations, finances, politics, religious beliefs, the car, the house, mother, father, girlfriend's, boyfriends, sports, music, television, past events, future plans and so on. Each day is filled with these mind created discussions that are repeated over and over and over. Most of the time without any awareness that we're having them. Television, movies and other forms of entertainment are filled with dramas that parallel this obsession of the mind to be anywhere but in the present. Our lives are inundated with this kind of noise and hence we become victims to it. It happens to all of us. It is the result of our conditioning, hence our nature and often the result of that noise is anxiety and stress.

We are conditioned to look at what is not happening and make it a happening. Consider all the things we prattle on about and think about as that which has happened and we can't do anything about or it is that which we think about that has not happened. Whatever it is it is not happening! And if it is not happening why is it so in command of our lives?

There is a world of not happening, happening but that world only exists in our minds. We bring into the reality of now that non-reality of then and allow it to find a significant place in our present. We give non-reality, reality and allow it to violate the beauty and splendor of our present moment. This moment in time is all that exists in that it is completely pure in every way until we crowd it with non-reality.

What is not happening ever really happens in the present. Even when we bring the thought of it into our present moment, it is still not happening. We just allow ourselves to feel as though it is as if that somehow shows the nobility of concern for coming events, or that our worry and concern is a preparation for what is not happening. It is the emotions we allow ourselves to feel and express, through all this not happening that damages us. Isn't it interesting how we have created ways to feel emotionally when we think about all the things that are not happening in our present state? It is one thing to feel in present time but to feel for that which is not happening is to allow the body and mind to obsess and weaken over things it can do nothing about. Consider that events or circumstances we create in our minds that are not happening, impact the health of our bodies in the present! Only the mind-created reality of non-reality is capable of doing this.

We all know that the brain is an incredibly complex instrument that controls and monitors every aspect of the human body. It is also the instrument of cognition, reason and emotion. It is a great instrument of learning and memory, sensory input and sensory filtering. We hear often that most humans only use five to ten percent of the brain's capacity to compute and store information. We often hear this in conjunction with the admonition that we are so much greater then we think ourselves to be. If somehow we could tap into this unused part of the brain and use it more fully we could achieve and be so much more than we are now. On a physical level this may be true but remember we are more than just physical beings. We are spiritual beings first, housed in physical forms. Our spiritual nature exceeds any physical concepts, thoughts or thinking of the human mind. Yet it is the physical that we focus on the most. The mind is part of the physical reality we live in and as incredible as we believe it to be we're still so much more than that. Even if we were using one hundred percent of what we consider to be the capacity of the brain we are greater than that. Right now in this very moment we exceed any thought or thinking the mind creates.

Why then do we allow ourselves to be run by our thinking? This is one of the great mysteries of our time. Even in new thought circles we fall back to the mind or the subconscious mind as the great gift of human beings. Most will acknowledge the spirit but rarely is the intelligence of the spirit acknowledged as something outside human intelligence. Human thinking has the benefit of our physical senses which are vivid and loud and our minds have concocted the idea that anything that cannot be observed in some way by these senses either cannot be real or, in some cases, is simply reconciled as impossible. The irony is that all of us at one time or another have experienced things for which our mental state, the mind, simply cannot explain and yet it is as real, sometimes even more real, then anything we have ever experienced through our other senses.

The mind holds rigidly to its reality by talking incessantly about everything it has created an identity with. That is how it reinforces its reality and it does this constantly. Often it is working under the radar of consciousness but it is always working. Inexorably it locks us into what it conceives as important. Its tendency is to over complicate things and make life an endless series of struggles and trials. So successful has the mind, and the collective mind, been at complicating our lives that we find ourselves in this realm of what's not happening believing it is what is happening. In fact, much of our new age thought has focused on the trials and struggles we face as opportunities for growth in the physical sense. Clever tool, the mind, to convince us that the only way out of its devices is to accept that struggle and suffering is for our benefit and that through such things life improves.

Three dimensional life is supposed to be fun and it should not be complicated and fraught with struggle as the mind imagines it. A mind that is constantly looking outward for answers to the struggles and suffering in life will always look to what's not happening for those answers. It will create scenarios outside the present moment that projects an outcome that is not happening. It may even look to the past and claim that we must learn from those experiences even though, they too, are not happening. It is all too easy to complicate the present with what is not present. It is the common state most of us find ourselves in. Even the law of attraction has been distorted to such a degree that our wanting or desires are a product of what's not happening. Put your intention out there and the universe conspires to provide it for you. The problem with this is that it plays directly into the mind-created reality that once you have what you desire from out there you will achieve happiness, contentment or whatever it is you seek. We see this, as well, with the new age movement to find our purpose in life, the finding of which is our only way to freedom and happiness. People struggle endlessly to find a reason for being here. Finding purpose is the new what's not happening!

The implication of finding or wanting something in life is perhaps the strongest indication of the minds success at keeping us disconnected with what is happening from what's not happening. As long as we stay mired in the out there, what's not happening, we will never discover the in here. The in here is the place where time stops and no sense of wanting or desires exist. Everything just as it is, right now, is incredible and what we are is all there is and that is everything! There ceases to be complications with what was and what might be. Simply peace with the now and what's not happening quietly falls away. We have now and it is now where we have fullness.

The out there is a fabrication of the mind. There is nothing out there that can help you, hurt you, frighten you, strengthen you, heal you, satisfy you, teach you, etc. All that is needed is already here. It is within us at any given moment. You already know it. You need only acknowledge it. I Am is always present. I met a woman who had become unemployed and was desperately trying to find work. On her way home from an interview one day she saw the billboard sign of a business she said she had passed every single day for several years. She mentioned that for some reason on this particular day the sign just jumped out at her in a way she had never seen it before.

She decided to stop and apply for work there without even knowing they were hiring. She went into the office and asked and the receptionist provided her with an application to fill out. The receptionist mentioned the company was hiring certain positions and asked the woman what she did. The woman responded with her particular skill and expertise and was told by the receptionist that is exactly what they were looking for. The woman filled out the application, attached a resume and handed it to the receptionist.

In telling the story the woman spoke as if something quite unknown to her was working inside her. She even said the words in describing the events, "you know law of attraction and all of that." She said everything was unfolding in ways she had never experienced before and she believed an inner force was working for her.

By the time the woman drove home she had a message from the company asking if she could come in for

What's Happening?

an interview the next day. She immediately called and arranged for the meeting. She was excited; you could hear it in her voice as she told the story. She expressed how everything had fallen into place and how she just knew that attraction was at work in her life. She explained that she knew things were aligning her way and that she had never in her life seen things so clearly. It was a compelling story. She went to the interview the next day with a feeling she had never felt before and just knew everything would fall into place. She was taken on a plant tour by the human resource manager who explained how committed the company was to its employees. The benefits were among the best in the industry and by what she saw everything about the company was wonderful.

She was interviewed by seven or eight people during the course of the day and taken to lunch by the Human resource manager, as well. She recounted how every single interview was so pleasant and how she hit it off with everyone she talked to. It couldn't have been a better round of interviews and her connection to everyone she met was, as she described, uncanny. She explained that things could not have aligned better and she said she knew Law of Attraction was working in her behalf. She knew this was a special place and would be a place she could call home. She just knew she would be offered the job.

As she continued telling the story she explained that she left the interviews feeling "up" in a way she had never experienced before over anything, much less a job. The next day the human resources representative called her to explain that everyone who interviewed with her thoroughly enjoyed her and thought she would be a perfect fit for the position and a welcomed member of the company family. The woman was ecstatic! Everything was so right and had fallen into perfect place, as she put it. The Human resource representative extended her the offer of employment with great hopes she would join the company and begin work as soon as she could.

Upon hearing the offer all of the sensations of alignment and connection stopped suddenly. She said that she was insulted by the offer. She said that even though salary requirements had not been discussed in the interview process she said she thought with how everything had gone up to that point that the "right" salary would fall into place as well. The offer was a few thousand dollars a year short of what she had previously made before being laid off. Rather than make a counter offer she told the representative she wasn't interested in the job at all. The phone call ended on that abrupt note.

Listening to this woman tell this story I couldn't help but think that she had completely missed the point of Law of Attraction. In fact, something far greater than the law of attraction may have been at play. It sounded like intuition had taken over the events of her life the previous few days and was guiding her down a perfect path. Higher powers were present and she knew it. Every door was opening but as soon as she heard their offer all the lights went out. She went back to all the things not happening, like her previous job and salary, and that became her happening! Instead of staying in the light she knew was guiding the situation she became insulted and offended because the company would dare make such an offer. Her "being offended" blinded her to even making a counter offer which likely would have been accepted. Her explanation was, "how dare they insult her the way they did." It was amazing to listen to her go from what appeared to be a spiritual high to an emotional low just in the telling of the story.

What's Happening?

I was saddened by the outcome of her story. I couldn't help but think of everything she would miss out on by not accepting the position. The friends made lifelong connections and a secure job with a company who would most likely have increased their offer if she had asked or raised her salary after a few months on the job. After all everyone loved her and she loved them. Families take care of their members and she had been accepted as a member before getting an offer to work there. I couldn't help but think of all the things aligning for her to have a perfect career with a company who would do everything to make her life more comfortable and enjoyable. All for naught because she was insulted.

We won't know all the circumstances of the story since it was only her recounting but it seemed to me that a lot of "what's not happening" was happening for this woman. Why the feeling of insult? Why not even a counter offer? Had past events in her life made her so sensitive that she would react in such a way? Was she going to be better off holding out for more money when up to now no offers had been extended? She lamented that she was soon to run out of her unemployment and she had no prospects. It is difficult not to make judgments about such a story but rarely have I listened to a story where the "bush" burned so bright. How much more do you need to be convinced you are being directed by the inner divine? Her life partner may have been working at the company or an acquaintance of one of her would be co-workers. There is no end to the possibilities she turned away from because she was offended. The light could not have burned brighter. At least in her telling of the story.

We can only speculate (what's not happening) as to what past events or future circumstances caused her to dismiss what she expressed at one point would be what she would do, e.g. work for this company.

Past events and future possibilities are not and never will be happening. They should never be brought into the reality of what's happening and what was happening for this young woman was a connection to higher light than she had previously known only to be shut off by some erroneous pull from the past into the nonexistent future. Light into darkness; happening into not happening!

It's just that; not happening. How often we let what's not happening become significant in our lives when what is happening right now is the only space we need to be present for. It is the human part of us that possesses this unique ability to make what is not happening into the consciousness of what is happening. Even our physical senses are overwhelmed by the power of the mind to create that which is not so. Somehow we must find a way to accept responsibility for what we intuitively know and never should we lose that knowing to past events in our lives that blind us to our inner awareness. Salaries, positions, recognition, awards, past and future events, etc. are all extraneous events we let cloud our inner knowing and the loss is tremendous.

We all need to let go of what's not happening and let what's happening be ALL that ever happens. Our true place in the world, "the ground upon which we are standing," is right now. It will never be any place else; neither should we.

Chapter 7

Duality – Monitoring Your Illusion

The egoic nature of man has become very sophisticated as the ebbs and flows of life change and alters with the times. We are living in a time some would call a spiritual awakening and individuals around the world are coming out of the proverbial woodwork to "awaken" or to help others to do so. It is a wonderful time to be alive and witness the outpouring of light and energy throughout the earth and it is happening in nearly every country on earth. Something is happening and it is wonderful. Ego sees this as well.

There is a nuance of ego that makes it so effective in its game of deception that most of us will never see it happening and go on deluding ourselves with whatever it is we have grabbed onto. The nuance of ego is that it creates its own counterpart to blend in with whatever cultural mood is taking place at the time, and it is so good at it that we actually believe we have found our inner self.

For instance, in the new age of spiritual awakening I alluded to earlier, a major part of spiritual awakening is about finding and connecting with the "inner self". I talk about this as well in the book <u>On Being God</u> and even make this inner identity the god of your experience. For those whose hearts have been opened to this new awareness, the ego subtly fools us into thinking that the part of us that is "connecting" to inner self is indeed the inner self. In its cleverness, ego even speaks the language of spirituality and we believe that that part of us is the newly found, enlightened part of us that was trying to find expression in our life. In its subtleness, this false identity proceeds to make everything we have or want in life okay.

Not that having or wanting are not okay, but one well-recognized spiritual leader of our time publicly expressed how nice it was that he could wear seven hundred dollar hand-crafted Italian shoes. He further expressed that he deserved such things, as do all of us, as if to make his desire to wear expensive hand-crafted shoes okay because collectively the rest of us who cannot afford such things "deserve" them. If I acknowledge that you deserve something but can't afford it that, somehow, makes it okay for me to have it because I can. Why would you say something like this? I don't understand this. If I but acknowledge your lack, albeit your deserving nature, I justify my "having". How does this help anyone? And yet this is a well-respected and great man who has done a tremendous amount to help thousands around the world.

"We all deserve" is an individual and collective indulgence, but it is also a part of the dual nature of the ego that dupes us into thinking we have found our spiritual nature when we have not. This is ego at its subtle best. God wants you to be rich is its mantra and you can have it all. Like Jesus being shown all the kingdoms of the world, including our own times, if he would but forsake his own soul. That is what ego asks of all of us. Look to me for everything and I will provide and ego continually dazzles us with new and improved enticements to keep us trapped in the illusion. And still our soul calls out and searches for more. Cleverly, the ego has convinced us that we should have the things it has collectively created and it is all ours if we forsake our own inner abundance. The price we pay is always too little but most of us hand it over eagerly. In fact, let's test how great our illusion is right now.

How real and unbreakable is your illusion of reality? The structures we have constructed for ourselves, individually and collectively, grip us in a way that reflects just how convincing our illusions about life are. We can sense the hold of illusion by performing this little thought test:

How strong is your illusion? If everything as you now know it was to be stripped away completely and you could reconstruct your life in any way you choose, what would it look like? How would your newly constructed life look in the face of this possibility? Please answer all of these questions honestly and don't hold back in any way:

- How would you be living? Remember you can put your life back together anyway you want. There are no limits and anything you want will be instantly yours. Again, how would you be living?
- What kind of work would you be doing or what career path would you choose? Would you be a senior member of your company's staff or would you have your own perfectly run company? You can "make it so" anyway you desire.
- What would your family look like? Perfect Mother and Father? In laws that you love or that never come around?
- How would your children be in this new creation of yours? Are they perfect angels; smart, bright, imaginative? Or maybe they are grown and changing the world in their own right.
- Who would your friends be or if you could choose the same friends, would they be different? Would you have more friends or would you have fewer. Would you change any of them or would the quality of your new friendships be different? Would you be different in your relationship with them?

- Where would you be living? Remember you can choose anywhere in the world and it is yours. Where is your "dream" place?
- What would your home look like? What would you add or remove from the home you are living in now.
- In America we speak of the "American Dream." What would your "American Dream" look like?
- What cars would you drive? Would you have more of them?
- Would you travel to foreign lands and vacation in exotic places around the world? Think of all the places you have always wanted to visit and enjoy. Do you have a "dream" vacation? Remember you will have whatever you can imagine!
- How would your financial situation look in this newly created reality? Would you have money in the bank, stocks, bonds, real estate holding such that you would never have to worry about financial things?
- What educational path would you have taken what degrees, honors, etc.? Pick your college, your credentials, honors or degrees. It is yours by simply thinking it. No limits!
- What organizations would you belong to?
- What social groups would you participate in; contribute your time and money to?
- How would you place yourself in your community? Would you actively participate in charities, church, schools, and other organizations where you believed you could contribute in significant ways? Would you do volunteer work, help the poor, etc.?
- How would you look and dress?

- Who would you know, or not know that you do now? Would your range of influence and social awareness be different than what it is now?
- What would the world look like in your newly created reality? What would government look like nationally, locally, etc.? How would international affairs be conducted and what, if any, part would you have in them?
- What things would you do that you don't do now?
- What things that you do now that you wouldn't do in this newly defined reality that you created?

    Make this about you and be as lavish, imaginative or creative as you can. There are no wrong or right answers to any of the above questions. In fact, many of the questions may be misleading or distracting from where your thoughts and ideas would like to go. Go anywhere you want. The importance of the exercise is to honestly look at your life as it is now and determine how you would reconstruct it if you could. Anything is possible in the creation of your new life and all we are trying to accomplish by considering all these things is how set in "your" specific illusion you are.

    Those who are honest will almost always assess these kinds of questions, and many more like them, and reconstruct their worlds along these lines. This is what we know, therefore these are the things we would tend to look at and change or improve if we could. In a lot of New Age thought, we are told that when we change our thinking, we can change our world. Much of that teaching tells us to identify our wants and to picture them and imagine with great emotion having anything we want. If a recapitulation of the past is unacceptable to you, consider those things you want and identify how such things would improve or better your life and circumstances.

Consider the things you have yet to achieve or desire at some point in your life. Much of our New Age thinking would have you focus your attention on such things as relationships, financial status, physical health, spiritual awareness, mental wellness among others. What do you desire in any of these areas? What do you focus on now that you want to have manifest in your currently reality? Let your mind go, even if you are certain none of these things will ever come about. It is the nature of your thinking we are looking at. The focus of your attention is key to understanding the complexity of your illusion. The personal intricacies of our lives and our dealings with family, friends, and acquaintances all factor in to how we view life. Our view of life is our illusion.

After giving some consideration to the reconstruction of your life and what it looks like in the new and improved version, compare it to the old. How is it different? Are you in a bigger house in a new location? Do you drive nicer cars? Do you have more money and freedom to do things you love, such as travel? Are you better educated? Is your career path moving in a new direction with higher position, more money and prestige? Do you participate in associations and charitable organizations? Are your children in the best schools with prospects for great futures? Are your relationships uplifting and fun and are you adored by family and other outside acquaintances? Are you fit and attractive regardless of age? Does the world make sense to you and are local and national governments doing everything exactly as you believe it should be? Are the stresses and complications you know now gone in this new life? Are you happier and more relaxed? Compare all the aspects of your newly created life with those you currently know. Now ask, "What is the difference between them?" Before continuing on really consider this newly described state you have created and how much improved your life is with all the things you have brought into your new reality. Breathe it in as if it had really happened and consider how you are feeling in this new place. Consider how much better life is now.

Now, in truth, what has really changed? For most of us, the difference can be measured in size, quantity or quality, relative to what currently is. A bigger house, more money, better relationships, etc. This is our, so called "new" illusion but it's really no different than the illusion we had before it! Our conditioning is so confining that we honestly believe that the extension of what we already know, what we already have in size, quantity and quality is what will make us happy and more content in life. We have accepted the myths that more money will give us greater freedom to do the things we want.

And what are the things we want? More of the same! A bigger, more comfortable house in the more exclusive neighborhood is still a house. The natural extension of this new dream house is an even bigger house in the mountains or on an ocean beach or perhaps a second house for the summer, or winter. Our conditioning has created the illusion that bigger is better. More of the same seems to be our motive to think ourselves into greater accomplishment or greater freedom.

We have even been conditioned to accept that greater accomplishment, more money, stature and position is the true meaning of success. Look how successful "so and so" is and we make that a marker for ourselves to emulate. "How to" books are written and the lives of the successful, as we have come to define them, are paraded in front of us as the model for how we should live our lives, and in so doing, we too can be successful. You can have manifested in your reality more things, credentials and wealth, and you will escape the travails of your current existence. Replace what you have and are with bigger and better versions of what is and you will be a success. Have or be anything you want. Visualize abundance as defined by the illusion you live in and you will bring it into existence. This is our illusion!

Here is what the illusion is not. There are no unsuccessful lives; No, not one! If we were to look at the life of Jesus in our terms today, he would be an abject failure. In gathering up his followers after his death, his apostles managed to find 120 people who believed in him. That is all he had to show for three years of absolute commitment to his teachings and hard work. Not to mention his ignominious death and burial. Buddha would be judged the same in our modern day terms. For Buddha, he was a royal prince endowed from birth with all the things we believe define success. He had it all and for some reason, he gave it all up to put himself in the midst of those who had nothing; or what we might define as the unsuccessful. By today's standards, some would say he gave up success to be a failure or that he could have done more if he had harnessed his wealth and put it to use to teach and spread his message. Most would, for sure, consider him to be crazy.

No one actually believes Jesus and Buddha were failures, yet the measure of value and worth we use to identify successful people today are the very things they put aside. If such things are the mark of success, then why would two of the most "known and influential" people in history completely fail to measure up to such standards? In fact, in the case of Buddha, why would he give up everything we define as successful after having it handed to him on a platter? These are unanswerable questions if you hold to a modern day definition of success.

Our egoic drive to create an image of success and to form a culture that recognizes earthly value, means, affluence, credential and all the other things we place such high value on, is exactly the opposite of what the Buddha and Jesus taught while they walked the earth. Neither of them sought fame, popularity or wealth and yet they lived abundant, rich and full lives. Lives on their terms. Their success was the awareness of the inner self and that awareness was their freedom.

Not the freedom we have come to define as "having means so we are free to do more" but exactly the opposite. Being free of means so they were able to "be" and consequently do things that in today's terms we call miracles and concede only they could do. Not doing more in the sense of being able to do things that give us earthly pleasure, but doing more to understand their own innate natures – their "being" which was that of gods. When we focus on the illusion of success we have created for life, we push away God. We are gods, so who is it really we are pushing away?

Success, as we have come to know it, is a highly egocentric, consequently illusory, idea we have created for collective society. In Western society, and more particularly in American society, we have even created a sort of arrogance that says that unless those of poorer circumstances are raised to the level of our definition of success, they cannot find the greater enlightenment we claim to have found. Hence the statement often heard that money or means gives us more freedom. In fact, it is now widely believed and taught that greater wealth provides more freedom. Freedom comes not in the attainment of those things we describe as successful, but in the letting go of all the illusory ideas about success we have come to accept.

"That which we hold on to holds us." The nature of ego is to accumulate, own and possess. In actuality, to truly have more freedom, we must learn to care less about the things we think freedom is and care more about what we believe it is not. Most of us believe that freedom is something we are given by a benevolent government or institutional authority that allows us to move more freely in society. We build militaries to defend our "rights" and protect our freedoms, believing that somehow freedom, having been given to us, must be protected and defended. In the political sense other collectives may try to take away that which we claim to be freedom, but the reality is that freedom is not a right we should expect to be handed to us or defended for us. The truth is we are free; always! Even under the arm of tyranny or abject slavery we are all free. We of our own free will give away our freedom to an illusion that anything in this life matters more than "who we are" outside anything we have or don't have.

The ultimate slavery, and exactly the opposite of our collective idea of freedom, is accepting that life comes with conditions or definitions we accept as true. Allowing your thoughts, your dreams, or actions to be outlined in the terms of those whom you have trusted through the course of your life, whether they be individuals or institutions, is real slavery and it is slavery of your own making. Ultimate freedom is not an inherent right to choose, it is however, to simply be that which you are outside any construct *you* have created for yourself. It is not what we are that restricts us. It is what we have come to think we are that does. Freedom is being the god that you are, and gods never make choices because they are free, by our collective definition, to do so.

When we say "we have the right to choose whatever we want" we are not describing freedom. We are describing the dual concept of choice that implies that something we have labeled as our right must be fought for, else we could lose it.

Freedom is not something that can be lost, or taken. Regardless of the condition we find ourselves in, or whatever walk of life we come from, we as gods are free. And no circumstance, power or condition can take that away from us. We often hear people, when referring to freedom, say something like "this is what I believe freedom to be" and then go on about what it is in three dimensional terms, including the ultimate right to make choices that affect their life situation. *Those who have choices have no freedom.* Living a life that is deciding the better of choices is a life of captivity and it only exists because we have allowed the illusion of our particular life to dictate a set of rules we choose to live by and call it freedom. Gods have no rules, thus no limitations and without limitations there is no choice that ever needs be made nor is there anything to be free from.

Ideology only exists in the human mind. In other words, it is a description or idea, we as humans create, of something that can only be described in human terms. Ideology does not exist in the realm of gods. Gods have nothing to defend and that is the ultimate freedom! Nothing is judged. The oppressor is just as enslaved as the oppressed when he must uphold his belief at the cost of suppressing others, while the oppressed enslave themselves by judging the oppression unfair or unjust. The two are not different and view freedom in only three dimensional terms. Freedom has nothing to do with choices and anyone who is in between two choices will not be free because he or she chose one or the other. Freedom comes not by choosing. It comes by being; knowing full well the extent of your own divine nature and knowing you are God frees you from anything that looks like a choice.

Choosing ties us to outcomes and leads to a succession of choices that, hopefully, lead up to that outcome. Being is never tied to outcomes and subsequently is free of any consequences we imagine deprive us of freedom. Freedom is really acceptance that our particular life is rich with experience that adds to our enjoyment as gods. We either move through life the victims of our choices or the recipients of a richness that accepts experience as nothing more than experience. In other words there are no right or wrong choices because choices do not exist. Freedom is knowing; knowing at the intuitive level that our lives are directed at a higher awareness than we allow ourselves to accept. True freedom is intuitive knowing. Choices are non-existent to the individual who recognizes their own divine nature. The only thing standing in the way of this knowing is our own conditioned lives that have us convinced that, not only do we not know, but that we cannot know.

Our reality is the product of what we have come to believe is important in life. Most of this belief, if we are honest with ourselves, was taught to us and is centered on the things others have taught us are important to maintaining a *safe*, life. The safe life asks that you accept the conditions of your experience and not extend outward too far, and by so doing you can expect reasonably predictable results. This is why when we are reassessing our so called wants we typically visualize or objectify bigger versions of what we already have or what others have that we would like to have in our experience. This is a safe approach and frees us from looking deeper within at the divine self that not only perceives more but sees that what we say we want is beneath the nature of our innate selves. The human moves toward safety, security and comfort while the divine moves toward adventure, richness and experience. The safe life is slavery.

We are greater than any experience or culmination of experiences yet common to our human nature is to subjugate ourselves to our experiences and determine that they are a pathway, to the greatness we know ourselves to already be. This is our greatest folly. Our illusion creates needing and wanting and both of these pull on a false duality that only exist because we see life as something out there that is needed in one sense and wanted in another. Ask anyone what they really want or what they really need and you will almost always get an answer that reflects a bigger and better version of what they already have. "I want a bigger house with a bigger kitchen or study, lots of bathrooms, bigger yard, etc." Or they may want a better job, more money and greater "freedom" to do and see things. It is part of the egoic deception that "having more, gives you more". In egoic terms, having more does give you more but it is just more stuff! It is more egocentric stimulus and the more you can acquire and possess the more adept you become at justifying it. And all it costs is your true spiritual nature.

In much of new age thought, the idea of gathering more has been extended to include purpose and meaning for life itself. There is a tremendous amount of energy being expended trying to find a reason for our being here in the first place. Finding this, for many, has replaced the gathering of *things* aspect of life, but has also taken on obsessive qualities. It seems many are letting go of the idea that they must gather things to them in favor of taking on more meaningful experiences that adds, so called, value to others.

Having and getting what's out there, whether it be shoes, cars, homes, wealth, acclaim or purpose, is always egoic. *Wanting is egoic.* Even wanting what our conditioning tells us is good and noble, such as "wanting to make a difference in the world" or other gestures to help or improve mankind. The reason it is egoic is that such "wanting" is driven by the illusion that our wanting for others what "we" think they need, want or, better yet, *deserve*, is our perception of how something should be out there. It has nothing to do with knowing who it is that dwells in us that is completely happy with everything that goes on in human experience. Who we are judges nothing; it loves everything!

Our wanting for others reinforces our illusion of what we have come to believe is what others want. We need to disconnect from what we want, or what we think others need or deserve and simply *act* because that is what the God within each of us does. It acts; that is all. It is difficult to comprehend this, because as soon as we determine what is best for someone, or decide what we must do for them, we invalidate them and ourselves as well. The god within each of us speaks to everyone regardless of how we define others physical conditions. We will all hear in our own way and respond from a place of inner knowing that will only concern us individually. It will be in this space that our reaching out will look compassionately on other gods experiencing life as they do and loving them fully regardless of their state.

None of us escape the illusion and those who seem to have mastered their lives and freed themselves from the "having," are never far from it. The pull of humanity is inexorable but that "being" that dwells within us sees no difference between the egoically created good or bad. Duality dissolves into living and experience without any judgments and it simply loves, appreciates and enjoys everything!

Chapter 8

Saviorism; Can You Really be Saved?

One of our greatest faith base deceptions and one that we all buy into in some form as humans is the mythology that something or someone is going to save us from whatever form of adversity we may face in our current experience. Throughout the ages humans have sought for outside sources to rescue us, or at least, to make fair what seems to be unfair in our existence. Judgment day and Karma are forms of this "making fair" scenario and most of our common mythological stories are rooted in the idea of saviorism. This idea rings in every aspect of our existence including our governments, local and national leaders, religious leaders, corporate leaders, etc.

No greater deception exists in human experience then the idea that we can and will be saved by some benevolent force that possesses power greater than our own. In fact, in our government and religious institutions we willingly hand over our own power as individuals so that they may save us from forces we believe we are unable to control. It has become more and more prevalent in western politics and that serves as a good example from which to illustrate this deception.

Regardless of our own individual politics, all government is seen as bad or good from the collective standpoint. Some faction sees the current leaders as their saviors while another faction sees it as doom and the cause of social problems whatever they may be. Both claim their own political saviorism as the way out of whatever dilemma they choose to embrace and blame the other as the cause for their existing problems. It is a vicious cycle which we, collectively, will never get out of because regardless of your political view no one can save us.

To use an example let's look at the phenomenon that occurred in America with the election of President Obama. Candidate Obama articulated an inspiring message to the American people and utilized social media to reach the electorate in unprecedented ways. His message of hope inspired people on every level of the population. Conservatives who would not think of voting Democratic in a presidential election did exactly that because they were so uplifted by the message of hope proffered by candidate Obama.

This breaking of ranks swept him into the presidency with a huge popular vote. Exit polls of voters from both parties spoke in fervent terms, saying they "believed" President Obama would bring a better day to the American landscape. In other words He could save us from the likes of his predecessor and all of his errant ways. It was a remarkable feat for President Obama to be able to whew so many into believing he could save us from the failures of the previous administration. But it took the idea of the collective that a savior was possible in the first place to make such an outcome happen. The people cried out, "we need a savior" and the response of the campaign of candidate Obama was, "I can save you."

There was a hope and enthusiasm amongst, not only Americans, but the world as a whole. New leadership followed by an era of prosperity and all eyes looked again to America as a leader in the world. Without making this a political statement all the expectation and hope, the freshness of a new and energetic president did not go as expected. In fact, after just a few years into the presidency the collective disillusionment was as great or greater than it had been with the previous administration. In just a few short years a growing collective cries out to be saved from him! What happened?

It is a timeless condition of the human experience. "Somebody save me!" Even with the full power of the President of the United States of America President Obama was remiss to save any of us from the perceived ills we see in the United States and the world at large and so we sit back, frustrated yet again. We say to ourselves, "I thought He was the one," but He wasn't. And so we look again for the next "savior" who may be waiting in the wings. We just know he or she is out there!

Religious institutions reflect the same kind of outward looking as well. Jews continue to look for another king David who will rise up and put down all the enemies of Israel and save them from a world that is set upon their destruction. At no time in history has any religious group looked more forward to a savior. Christians, too, look to the returning Jesus so save them and the world from those who do not believe in him, as their personal savior." The great saving device of this returning God is his swift and righteous judgment, righting all the wrongs Christians the world over have suffered.

For Muslims, Allah, will vindicate the faithful and restore the birthright they, too, believe was taken from them. Hindu's and Buddhists will cycle around in different forms until they have satisfied the requirements of God whose rules they subject themselves too. Their savior is time; endless time.

Religious institutions the world over whether they be large collective movements, small and localized, mystical, dogmatic, new age or old age all look to some force out there to equalize and make right what they collectively perceive as unfair or wrong. All that is asked of the individual is to believe that the unique collective perspective will be right. In other words, suffer now with patience and hope and ultimately you will be vindicated. There is no difference whether the collective institution is secular or religious. They all cry, "We are right and they are wrong." People go to their graves with this kind of hope, believing everything they were taught was wrong will be righted!

Human history is littered with fallen saviors who came with the power of words and ideas but failed to provide any long term solution to the plight of people or nations. In fact, history is nothing more than an endless parade of one thing not working but being overcome supposedly by something better only to fail and repeat over and over again. Winston Churchill referred to history as "just one damned thing after another." How very true.

If we can learn anything from history it is that we cannot learn from history! What we should gather from history is that nothing, no one, can or will save us. No president, political party, nation, religion, individual, philosophy or ideal can save us. We cannot be saved because there is nothing to be saved from!

Somehow the human mind, the ego has convinced us that we all need something outside of us to make us whole and complete. To protect us and make our lowliness or lack in the world a cause for equalization by some force that has power beyond our own. We are conditioned throughout our lives to accept some form of saviorism. It is as if the ego is hiding from some great unknown crime for which it must pay by accepting an outside force to resolve. It seems that the reality we all accept on some level is that guilt unworthiness, evil, etc. is the state of human awareness. It is not always aimed at our individual selves. These characteristics are often aimed at those who are not like us. Thus the collective finger pointing for our own collective ills.

Saviorism is dependency. It stems from the fear we are taught throughout our lives that we are to be perfect even though no one can describe perfection without their own unique judgment of it. We convince ourselves that no one can be perfect and that being the case the idea of needing saving is automatically formed. The idea is so pervasive it inserts itself into every aspect of our lives. It lies at the root of the karmic idea that "what goes around comes around." "Sooner or later you will get yours" even if we have to wait a long time for it to happen. God, e.g. savior will make it right in the end.

Our saviors, consequently, take on many forms. They are people, places and things. Even pills and plants save us. For instance, we look for a pill to slim us down or prevent us from overeating. Heaven forbid we simply take control of our own lives and stop eating or start eating in ways that are healthier! Instead, someone will create a pill that lets us eat anything we want and as much as we want without becoming overweight. Perhaps the pill will come along that will motivate me to work out so I can get that body I have always dreamed of! Perhaps our savior is this new job I've been expecting that will launch both a new career direction and greater prosperity.

I have a friend who is partially disabled who lamented constantly that he could not be whole until his government disability was approved. Now that his disability has come through, which was more than he anticipated; he now complains that he cannot live on the amount provided even though he does nothing to manage the money he does receive.

Can you see the subtlety of it? My friend was saved from a story he created and now he has created a new story that the amount of disability is not enough. He is now looking for a new savior to rescue him from this latest unfairness. After that a new unfairness will lurk into his awareness and he will turn to yet another savior. "If I can just win the lottery it would save me from my financial burdens." I hold to my religious beliefs accepting fully my struggles, my faith will cause God to look favorably upon me and vindicate my lowliness.

We all do this. The greatest saviors we look to are governments and religions because they attempt to right all the wrongs on a much larger scale but the nature of saviorism permeates every aspect of life and it affects everyone of us regardless of our situation or circumstances. The most subtle are our most benign daily wants and desires, particularly our relationships. How many times have we heard someone proclaim, "Oh I can't live without him or her?" Or "I just won't be able to go on if they break up with me," etc. As if life without someone could save us from life altogether!

So many of our individual stories and dramas are played out because of the insidious control our minds play that we must have something or someone in place that will make everything better. This is saviorism! It even finds its way into new age thought that tells us that we can have anything we want if we put our focus and attention onto something even though the original premise is I can be saved from the lack I now have in my life by thinking about and working toward whatever it is I lack.

"Ask, and it will be given" is a common idea in our collective thought and yet at its core is that whatever it is you ask for will only come from some outside source to whom we are all beholden. That is saviorism. In fact, the subtle implication is that all you need to do is ask and something greater than you will provide it. This thing, whatever you call it, is the kind giver of that which you do not have. It will save you from what you do not have presently.

The only way out of this condition is to accept full responsibility for everything in your life. You create your existence and you, therefore, are your own savior should a savior ever be required, which when you take control of everything in your experience will never happen! There is nothing to be saved from in the responsible life. Taking responsibility for life is recognizing that nothing in human experience is personal to you even though it may seem to be.

We create our own experience and exist only as humans for a short while that will never be anything more than the experience. When we take this kind of control over our lives we see that everything that happens is unique and wonderful even if the collective world comes to our rescue and tells us "it's not right or good." It is said that "we must be the change we see in the world." In other words, until we decide that nothing outside our own unique existence can or need save us this idea of saviorism will haunt us for the entirety of our lives. It never matters what the world thinks of us or how we view ourselves in it. Nothing that happens needs outside forces to square our experience with anyone else's or with collective thoughts and intentions.

You are the hero of your life. I am the hero of my own. There is nothing that will save you simply because you are the hero, the savior and when we all remove our judgments of the experience we each individually enjoy something unique and special that no other can or will. That is the beauty of discovering the divine within us. It knows that this experience is nothing in infinity and is only to be enjoyed as only gods can. It also knows that there is nothing in infinity from which we can or need be saved. We literally have it all. We literally are ALL!

Chapter 9

Creative Responsibility

We are responsible for life! However, much of our reality is caught up in making others responsible for what happens to us instead, especially if what happens causes a disruption of normal life. In terms of our "life" experience as humans, we are equipped with two, often conflicting, abilities. The first is our intuitive knowing. That is, the part of us that understands our place in the universe as the God of our experience and the creative center of the universe. While resident in our physical bodies, it is aware of its higher order of existence. It might be called the God that we are, but know not.

The second part is our mind. The mind is the creator of reality on this three dimensional plane. It is the creator of the ego part of us that must identify somehow with everything we perceive and even many things we do not. The mind is what takes over the intuitive nature we all possess and attempts to clarify everything in terms it understands. For the most part, the world of human existence is mind created. The mind has the amazing ability to imagine things greater than what it observes and perhaps even understands and cause things to manifest in its reality. This accounts for the great achievements of mankind throughout history, and accounts for many of the things yet to be achieved. The mind has the ability to resonate vibrationally through thought, feeling and emotion and cause to appear in reality what those thoughts feelings and emotions focus on. In other words, we, as humans, can create our experience in the world in the terms of our human thinking and have pretty much anything we desire and set our minds upon. If the thoughts (energy) emanating from our minds vibrate at the level of "having" whatever we want, then we can achieve it. This is what has come to be known in New Age thought as the "Law of Attraction."

Everyone knows the part of the law of attraction that tells us that like attracts like. We even have more scientific descriptions that tell us that energy vibrates and that the rate of vibration is what makes things what they are. For instance, the rock is a rock because its vibration is not the same as that of the tree or bird or whatever form matter has taken. Everything in the universe is energy vibrating at different frequencies such that all forms appear to be different from each other. In the vibrational sense, this is true but in the energetic sense, it is not. Everything is the same at the base level of existence. All that is different from one form to the other is the frequency at which energy vibrates. As it relates to the law of attraction, like vibration attracts like vibration. If our thoughts vibrate money and wealth then we will have money and wealth or if we vibrate stamina and health that is what we will have in our experience. That is how law attraction is said to work.

The aspect of law of attraction that we almost always overlook, even most teachers of it, is that while like attracts like, the manifestation of outcomes always comes in its own way. The universe is infinitely abundant and the giver of all things, but the way in which it gives is also infinite. No two creations are ever the same. How things manifest is the sole discretion of the universe. It gives freely and abundantly, but it always controls "how" whatever shows up appears to us. This is the point we tend to forget when we look at accepting responsibility for everything in our lives. Most of us never ask why we bring something into our particular existence, especially when we perceive it as bad, harmful or painful. Other than appearing in our experience we never acknowledge that we created it, whatever it is. Things don't happen for any particular reason. They happen because we create them. We bring them into our experience as a part of mind created experience.

In truth there is no "law of attraction." I know this is contrary to the new age thinking of today but in the reality of our experience outside the physical limitations we impose upon ourselves there are no laws. There are no rules. There is only infinite existence and in infinite existence nothing constrains anything else. Law of attraction sets before us choices that do not exist in infinity and puts the responsibility for a bad life or a good life on our physical awareness and energetic vibration. In reality forces we cannot imagine always underlie our physical experience. These are forces that we all possess but have been disconnected from because we have given away our higher awareness to lesser powers of which Law of Attraction is a part.

Being disconnected from our higher divine natures, we often fail to see our complicity in the events and experiences of our lives especially those of an unpleasant nature. It is the ego's way of having "plausible deniability" when things don't go as we expected them. In fact, ego is quick to explain why things don't go the way we think they should have. In most cases, it is because we did not plan correctly or execute the plan we created or that we did not take correct action. That tends to a biggie for the ego. Plan your work and work your plan. Working the plan, however, is fighting against a basic premise of The Law of Attraction. That is the premise that the "how's" are the domain of the universe. The "hows" are something our thinking will never control because the universe is the sole determiner of how things are to come about. We only need choose the "what" and align ourselves to it. In other words, vibrate to whatever it is and whatever action we take is correct action. If we are aligned to what we desire, any action in life will do. All that is necessary for us is to align with the "what" and take any action and it will manifest in its own way and time, often to our great surprise.

That is how law of attraction is said to work. Ask and it is given. The form, in which it is given, however, is where we get confused and begin to deny that what we experience in life is what we have attracted into it. It is wise but difficult to pay attention to the coincidences in our lives because it is they that give us a glimpse into something greater going on in our existence. Most of us have lost our intuitive abilities in favor of the more obvious five sense constructions we have come to accept as reality. The Law of attraction falls into this category. Another way to look at it might be to say that we are gods having a three dimensional human experience, but that the human has become the more dominant aspect of that life. How many of us really know when we hear the voice of God?

In spite of our human-ness, and the loss of knowing that we are divine, every inquiry, every supplication is responded to by our inner divine self. We ask and it is given every time without exception. Most of us, however, forget what it is we asked for while we are watching the answer manifest before us. In the spiritual realm, there are no coincidences. Coincidences only happen on the physical plane of reality we currently exist in. When we are closed off of our spiritual nature, we do not recognize that every coincidence is, in fact, a spiritual answer to a question or desire we expressed in a passing thought, a verbal exchange or emotional outpouring. There are no accidents in life, and spiritually speaking there are no coincidences. We create every aspect of the life we live.

For many, when looking at the so-called pitfalls, or the hardest of times in life, it is a hard thing to accept that they created it, that they are responsible for it. Especially when in the depths of despair, we are unable to see past, the circumstance manifested, to the nugget of truth and profound wonder that is right there in front of us. Most of us forget what it is we desire in the face of the answer before us.

Here's an example. Say that we have been very successful in our career such that we have access to pretty much anything and everything we could possible want in life. We have "the car" and toys and money to travel anywhere in the world and yet we feel empty and sad for some reason. We ponder for a moment if only we would somehow, some way, be happy. Nothing more than this thought and we pass it off and return back to our everyday life without ever considering it again. Months later we receive a call in the night telling us that we must evacuate our home immediately as a wildfire is bearing down on our particular neighborhood and our life is threatened. The evacuation is mandatory, so we gather the children, some clothes, some odds and ends and jump in the family car, and head over to friends or to another shelter that has been provided. A few days later, we are able to return to our home only to find it has been destroyed. Everything is gone.... Everything! What's worse, it is the only house on the block that has been taken. All others are unharmed. As you stand there looking in awe and disbelief, what thoughts begin to go through your head? Do you begin to wonder, why me? Are you filled with anger or grief at your poor, unfortunate state and do you blame God or some evil force for taking all that you worked for?

Certainly if someone came up to you in this terrible moment, and said "You created this, it's your responsibility" you would be enraged, angry, sullen and any number of other emotions, but the last thing you'd be thinking is that you created this. How could anyone ever want this in their life experience? Who wouldn't react this way? We don't ask for these specific things to happen to us, but we do ask that things in general do.

Remember that the universe owns the "how" in every creation. It is not for us to create the "how", only the "what". Remember the passing thought about happiness? Now, it is difficult to buy into the idea that losing everything you have will bring you happiness, but what about it? You threw the thought out there and went back to the life you were unhappy in. In fact, that unhappy life you built blinded you to any other thoughts about being happy. The universe responds. Always, without fail, but also as it sees fit. Let's look at this more closely.

You are living a life you once thought was the best possible way to bring about joy and happiness in your life. In fact, in everything you did, you were successful and it added to the things you could have, the places you could go. Every heart's desire supposedly being met except one and in a moment of pondering, you put into the universe the idea that your life remained sad and the quiet supplication to find happiness. Later, without ever considering such a thing again, you lose everything you owned in a fire. Remember everything you owned was not contributing to your happiness even though you continued to work hard to have it all. In an instant, it is gone and you are in despair – for what appears to be good reason! Many, if not most of us would never look at such an event as anything other than a disaster even though the universe's response to our creation was to take from us all the things we thought brought happiness but didn't. It removed them from our field of view in such a way that maybe, just maybe, we examine our life in another way.

Too often, the things we identify with in life cloud the things we should be identifying with. For many of us we would never be able to divorce ourselves from the awful tragedy of losing everything and surely not take responsibility for it. It was, after all, an act of God or happenstance that just took mine and no one else's.

Until we can comprehend that in the spiritual realm, the realm we are all a part of, there are no coincidences. Everything happens for a reason and more specifically, it happens for reasons we create. The saying "be careful what you wish for" rings true here even in those quiet moments when we consider that we actually do create our reality. Every aspect of it is ours to own and be responsible for. It's always easy to take responsibility for our lives when things fall into place and everything goes smoothly, but turn it around to disruption, chaos, loss and pain and it can't possibly be related to us. When we stop thinking in terms of life happening to us, we will begin to see how great our creative power is. We are gods, after all, and gods create!

For most of us, law of attraction is something we can wrap our minds around when things all seem to fall into place. Should things not be going as we thought then it is because of wrong thinking – easy, right? Law of Attraction is always connected, to worldly things and yet there is something far greater inside us that is really in control which most of us no longer know or accept. This is the true creator of our existence and it resides within us each and every moment of our lives. Our deepest thoughts and desires do not resonate from the mind but from inner knowing. The place where the god we are dwells is the place from which our happiness emanates. It is the place from which our godlike natures speak which unfolds as the creation of our experience. It is the place of no fear and no story. It is the place of knowing that resides in each of us and confirms what we all once knew very well. We are the creators of the Earth upon which we stand and that we are not the physical bodies we possess. We are something else that is pure and divine that dwells within these bodies for a short time only.

Each of us needs to reconnect to that otherness we all know we are and in so discovering recognize that the events of life are never personal. We are born into the circumstances of physical experience of our own creation and choosing and no part of the experience is to reshape or remold us into something we are or are not. All we have to do is find that part of us that loves every aspect of everything going on and all our judgments disappear and the richness of life experience begins to overwhelm us in spectacular ways. Responsibility for life is really acceptance of everything going on in life and acceptance is falling in love with the experience and nothing else. No part of life needs to be held accountable to our judgments about its fairness because every aspect of our existence is fair. In fact, the question of fairness doesn't even exist in a spectrum of infinity. It simply is ours for the experiencing and sheer enjoyment of the god like nature we all possess. The experience of life is never responsible to us in any way. We are responsible for it!

Embrace life and live with reckless abandon. Be life rather than a judge of it and it will open your senses in ways very few ever experience. We are life!

Chapter 10

Stream of Life

Follow a stream from its highest point, whether it is a spring releasing water from an unknown source or from the snows of winter melting and giving their life giving waters to everything below. As the stream finds its way down from its heights, it passes by or over many obstacles along its way, but it always seems to find a way. Its course often seems impossible, but as it runs into obstacles, it finds the path of least resistance which sometimes means going around obstacles or perhaps it waits patiently to fill a certain low spot that will allow its waters to eventually flow over its would-be obstruction. As we follow the stream, it will sometimes rush in great torrents down steep hillsides or spill over high cliffs into pristine pools below. Sometimes it will meander through large open meadows where beautiful alpine flowers bloom and fill the landscape with color, fragrance and brilliance. Perhaps the stream splits off and fills the meadow with small tributaries that merge back together. The sounds of the stream also tell us something about its travels in that it will gurgle as it meanders through unobstructed fields and meadows, but it rushes and roars as it surges over cliffs, down steep canyons filled with large boulders and other obstructions. As we continue our journey following the waters, we might see another stream joining ours, increasing its size and power. Still, the waters push forward, twisting and turning as needed to work its way around the landscape as effortlessly as possible. In fact, as we observe this stream, it never occurs to us that the waters are fighting their way downward. It all seems so effortless and easy. Even in those places where the river has cut its way through rocks and cliffs that, when looking at, simply does not look possible.

The stream weaves its way through a tapestry of life introducing us to all manner of trees, shrubs, plant life, and animal and insect life of all kinds. Some of the places the stream takes us are shaded from the sunlight and are cool and dark, even forbidding, while other places are sunlit and brilliant and the shadows cast on the moving water make it look different, even mesmerizing. There are places on its journey where it shoots through cracks in the rock and we see rainbows cast so close, we can touch them or we feel the cool mist on our faces. Everything about this journey is peaceful and calm and the constant rushing of the river soothes us and at times we may even find ourselves talking to the waters as if they could hear. They can!

Never do we sense, as we journey alongside the stream, that it struggles to get where it is going. It moves effortlessly, inexorably passing by all the wonders of its long journey to get to its destination which, by the way, does not exist. As it passes by life, it gives life by giving of itself so that all is refreshed, nourished and uplifted. It is a relaxed life that looks for peace wherever it goes, and it goes where it goes simply because that is where it goes. We may find evidence along the way when it changed course or with the help of natural forces it moves out of one bed and into another. Still, it matters not. The stream is not choosing a path to follow. It is simply flowing and as it flows, the path opens up, and with each new opening, new adventure, new beauty and wonder lies before it and it brushes up against all of it, content to take it all in and give back what it can in the form of life giving water.

Onward, ever onward, it moves through hills and valleys, forest and fields. Taking in but giving back. The stream gives life, but is given to life as life is given to it. Its course is never straight nor is it narrow or wide. We cannot map its exact course because a map of the stream's journey could never account for every detail the stream encounters on its way down the mountain.

The stream does not choose this way or that. It simply flows where the grade of the mountain (life) takes it and it embraces and gives back to everything it encounters on its way. Every aspect of the journey is just that – part of the journey. There is no purpose other than to serve as that part of the journey. That incredible moment is as the water passes by all that matters and all is uplifted and better for the experience. No great crossroads or turning points in this encounter or that one. Just life giving of itself for all to marvel at and enjoy. The stream moves on, as do we.

There are no perfect geometric patterns in life as we all would like to believe there is, or as our math and science teachers say. The straight path does not exist except in our imagined lives. There is no straight way to any purpose we consider to be our very own. Life is a stream! We are taught from a very early age that the shortest distance between two points is a straight line, but no part of our life on earth is a straight line. In life, the shortest distance between two points is the one that took you from point A to point B regardless of what distance you traveled or the time it took. Ego looks at life in a finite way, and in so doing, it must find order and structure that was never intended to be there.

Our true life is an infinite experience and every twist and turn, the ebbs and flows, as we call them, are never consistent with what our egos expect. This is the cause of suffering in individuals as well as in society. Ego constructs a true and ordered life and even uses sacred writings and ancient wisdom to reason with us that if we follow the prescribed path it reasons is the correct one, life will work out and flow effortlessly to the end. Those who rigidly follow their ego's prescribed course often find themselves in turmoil and needless suffering because they followed the rules and they didn't get where they were supposed to.

Life is full of Monday morning quarterbacks looking back at what went wrong with their plan or what they could have done differently to achieve the pre-planned outcome. We see this second guessing, questioning in every aspect of our lives including religion, academics, and occupations. We might hear someone exclaim, "I followed God's laws as I have been taught them", or "I worked hard and did everything I was supposed to, but why was I not protected or spared an outcome I was sure could not happen if I obeyed all the rules."

Unlike the natural flow of the stream which always finds its way, many will push against the natural course of life. They will push against it and question their misfortune. You can almost see them standing in the stream facing upward with clenched fist defying the direction of flow as if challenging it to reverse its direction and go where they command it. All it does, however, is move forward, following its natural course, either moving around you as you fight against it, or sweeping you up in its current. *Life does not care about the choices we make.* Life, like the river, flows on, embracing everything in its path, and giving back every step of the way.

If we could see our lives as a river or stream and simply flow with it, our journey would be so much more pleasant and our expectations would not get mixed up or confused with the twists and turns in life we could not see coming. The grand part of life we can all enjoy is the pure experience of it. A river has no purpose other than to flow where it will, and it is the same for us. Life flows on whether we resist it or not. Why not enjoy it?

Human ego is so busy finding or giving meaning to the process of life and finding justification and cause for everything that happens that we miss much of its inherent beauty. We pass by the works of man or nature and never see them because our focus is on understanding life rather than living it. In trying to understand it or analyze it, we miss it or it passes us by. Every bend in the stream, every change in direction is an opportunity to experience life in a new and incredible way, and particularly from our own unique perspective.

Maybe we won't experience things as others might, but what we do experience is uniquely ours and the only enrichment we need take from any experience is our own to appreciate and fully embrace. "What happens; happens." Not because we have control over life by the choices we make, but because there are no wrong choices, which is the same as saying there are no choices at all. If we participate in life without the mental anguish of deciding the better of all our various choices then anything we do, any path we follow will be good and right and un-judge-worthy. This type of participation in life removes the resistance we feel as well.

I used to tell my daughter, who would work so hard to get cast in school plays, or achieve academic success only to be disappointed over and over, that life was not fair. I would tell her that she would encounter situations throughout her life that would prove that life was unfair and that she would be mistreated along the way, even though she worked harder and harder to achieve her objectives. How naive I was and, unfortunately, the message I imparted to her was completely wrong. Not only

Stream of Life

is life fair, but it is completely honest. Life is truth therefore it cannot be dishonest. The only dishonesty in life is our own dishonesty which culminates deep within the egoic structures of the mind.

Our egoic identity is the only thing on this planet that resists the natural flow of life, to the point that what we have come to believe about ourselves and what we are is the only dishonest thing in life. Ego-constructed reality and reality are diametrically opposed to each other and we get caught up in the game of life that convinces us that life is hard and not always just or fair. Ego is always swimming against the current of life, trying to offer another kind of reasoning for the ebb and flow that doesn't always seem so pleasant.

Life is always honest and it always finds the way to bear that out. How hard we sometimes struggle to keep what we know about ourselves from ever seeing the light of day, and so we bring dishonesty to the light of life. Our lies, our dishonesty dims the light of life, and compounds our struggle against the stream that, if we would only let go of everything we hold so tightly to, would all drift out of sight and our lives would freely and effortlessly blend together with the flow of life never to be consumed in worry, doubt or the endless game of making ourselves "other" than ourselves.

Nothing in our three dimensional awareness can account for what is really happening and therein lies the greatest lie we tell ourselves. The more precise and defined we become, the less aware we are; and the more we convince ourselves that we are precise and defined, the more of our true selves we trample under foot, and the greater our lie becomes.

The lack of awareness culminates in the denial of the stream of life we all follow. It is to convince ourselves that we can make the stream of life straight and exact according to geometric rules that only hold in a manmade reality. We convince ourselves that within the sterile structure of manmade forms is the answer to who we are if we but push science to find the one simple equation that defines everything we will ever need to know.

Only the ego could have created such a lie. Only ego could convince us that straight lines can be found in nature and that a formula can be derived that will be able to predict everything we can expect for the future and give an explanation for everything that has happened in the past. Conscious awareness is a very limited awareness because of its ability to dump so much information so quickly we cannot even sense that it is happening.

As we meander or tumble through life, we tend to miss the incredible sights along the way as they are happening, but we know they were there because we think back upon them. Sometimes we look forward to the horizon out yonder and think that when we get there, things will be so much better, or all our questions will be answered. We easily look forward and backward because those are the places we can most freely and successfully lie about. In the conversation we have with ourselves, we can reminisce how much better things were "back then" or how much better they will be in some future "when".

Now, the present moment we exist in right now, is an honest moment that is pure and untainted by any thought for yesterday or tomorrow until our egoic reaction to it poisons it with untruth. Facing the present is our most daunting challenge because of its purity. In our un-pure state, we have difficulty facing the purity of present reality because being present forces us to look at ourselves without the ideological masks that we have created to shield us from the glare of present reality. Being present strips us clean of all the false definition we use to demonstrate ourselves to the world. It is a scary place for the ego. In fact, it is a place the ego cannot exist in because ego is anything but honest.

Ego needs identity. That is why it always reminds us and everyone else of its past accomplishments or projected future achievements. These are its cover; a safe haven from something that cannot be explained in its terms, its language.

The stream of life is infinite. The egoic life is finite. The two cannot co-exist. They cancel each other out. Either we are in the flow and completely truthful or we are in illusion and living a lie. The stream of life is enjoined with the world and nothing is missed along the way. The largest of egos and the highest degrees of knowledge and education cannot describe what the stream knows. Its world is the whole world and it is one with it. It knows the terrain, the hills, valley and rocks along the way and is never fooled by images condensed and printed on a map that the ego provides. It feels everything and reaches out to everything, as it gives to life, its "own" life.

Consciousness cuts away so much of life while ego tries so hard to convince us that what we are conscious of is the real nuts and bolts of life. It works hard to convince us that its view of the world "is" the world. Its view is always looking backward or forward, but never does it acknowledge the present with its billions and billions of pieces of information discernible right now to a quiet non-egoic soul.

We are in the stream of life whether the egoic self believes it or not, and the stream always moves ahead, even if we fight against the current. Our experience is an unfolding. The more we flow with life, the more a part of us life becomes. Every aspect of the terrain we pass through is our guide, our map and our journey becomes an infinite stream of intuition and awareness that consciousness no longer blots out. Our intuition and our wonderful bodies are sensory instruments available to all of us to navigate and enjoy our life experience here on planet earth.

We step off the cosmic train for a short time and we can enjoy the experience or fight against it. We choose. The ego created world is calculated and sterile and does everything it can to reduce the stimulation we all are equipped to comprehend. Granted, the comprehension is not in the language of ego, which has also been stripped away of the greater part of knowing. Our intuitive abilities need to be at the forefront of our awareness, not in the background as they often are. Tune them in and turn on the truth of real life. Real existence! Destiny is unknown, therefore, non-existent. The possibilities available to us along our journey through life are endless. Ego wants to see and plan for the end. It seeks a goal, an end that, when reached, is somehow a utopic conclusion to a well-planned life strategy.

I was speaking with a friend one evening who was looking for a catalyst of perhaps thought or an individual such as Buddha or Jesus, who by their words and deeds could change the hearts and minds of people to live in peace. He shared his thoughts about how the so-called age of enlightenment some 500 years earlier, which was ushered in by such great minds as Newton, Descartes, Pascal and others, had failed to provide the predicted "know how" to change a dark world into an enlightened one. The age of enlightenment was supposed to find "mind made" solutions to all the ills of human existence, including war, poverty, education, government, and every other aspect of life. My friend recognized the failure of the intellectual mind or so-called "enlightened mind" to accomplish anything other than to increase suffering and the carnage of war on a greater, more massive scale.

While he lamented this failure of enlightened minds to solve complex world issues, he asked me, "If the age of enlightenment is not the answer, what is the catalyst, event or individual that brings about changes the enlightenment sought but could not produce?" My answer was not what he wanted to hear. I told him that to look, in any way, to an outward cause, to an individual, or event would never bring about the changes in human existence he sought. The only change or catalyst he could ever affect was his own. I told him that we, as humans, are all a part of the stream of life, but that we each are our own stream as well. Individually, we affect the larger stream, but with human reasoning, we will likely never see it.

When we become our own catalyst, our change, we become the larger stream and it becomes us and our outlook on the conditions of the world we wish were different becomes part of a compassionate whole. When such a change takes place in us individually, everything else changes as well. My friend listened thoughtfully, but was unable to see it. His mind was convinced that something big and extraordinary was needed to alter things in the world as we know it. My response to him was that an individual transformation to higher awareness is big and extraordinary, but he would not accept that as an answer. "There must be something," he mused.

I could not help him. The majority of us look for the same thing. We look to our gods, our leaders, our parents, someone, anyone or anything that will reverse the way things are in a massive and dramatic way. We are conditioned to be this way. Heaven forbid we allow ourselves control of our own lives. That is how it was in the so-called enlightenment, when highly sophisticated and educated men determined that they could figure out anything intellectually. It continues to be a myth in the present day, yet the stream flows onward, ever onward and as long as we look for the utopic conclusion, the life strategy or catalyst that changes in a massive way those things we have determined must change we swim against the current of life. Life is, at that point, a struggle and we will never win against it. Despite our struggle and good intentions, we will be washed away in the inexorable flow of life that always moves forward. Everyone is eventually swept away in the current of life. Some hang on until the very end while others stop resisting and glimpse the beauty and splendor that is always there if we simply let ourselves get caught up in the flow.

The stream of life simply is! So too is life. Life is about being in the flow, not having or fighting for or against it. Regardless of the things we determine to be important, or the causes we choose, we struggle against or go with the stream of life but it always flows onward to an infinite destination we will never know. But we need not know because such knowing will not add one thing to the incredible beauty, abundance and wonder of our existence. We need only breathe life as it breathes us and go where it takes us.

There is no end in infinity! The stream of life is eternal life; so are you!

End

Afterword

Don't run around this world looking for a hole to hide in.

There are wild beasts in every cave! If you live with mice, the cat claws will find you.

The only real rest comes when you are alone with God.

Live in the nowhere that you came from, even though you have an address here.

  Rumi

Remember…YOU are God as "Human Being"

Be sure to visit Carl's website at: www.spiritual–intuition.com for all the latest information about spiritual transformation and awakening to new awareness.

You can also download a free copy of the E-book "Are You Listening? Addressing the Divine Within" when you sign up for the Spiritual Intuition Newsletter.

Look for Carl's newest and first novel titled: "Shaman" to be out in 2013.

For more information or questions regarding this book or any other spiritual needs please send an email to: carl@spiritual-intuition.com. We'd love to hear from you

Namaste